VALUES BASED
STRATEGIC PLANNING
A Dynamic Approach for Schools

VALUES BASED STRATEGIC PLANNING
A Dynamic Approach for Schools

Terry Quong
Allan Walker
Kenneth Stott

PRENTICE HALL

Singapore   New York   London   Toronto   Sydney   Mexico City

Published in 1998 by
Prentice Hall
Simon & Schuster (Asia) Pte Ltd
317 Alexandra Road
#04-01 IKEA Building
Singapore 159965

Prentice Hall, Simon & Schuster offices in Asia: *Bangkok, Beijing,
Hong Kong, Jakarta, Kuala Lumpur, Manila, New Delhi, Seoul,
Singapore, Taipei, Tokyo*

Printed in Singapore

5   4   3   2
02   01   00   99

ISBN 0-13-081926-3

Simon & Schuster (Asia) Pte Ltd, *Singapore*
Prentice Hall, Inc., *Upper Saddle River, New Jersey*
Prentice Hall Europe, *London*
Prentice Hall Canada Inc., *Toronto*
Prentice Hall of Australia Pty Limited, *Sydney*
Prentice Hall Hispanoamericana, S.A., *Mexico*

Contents

SECTION 1 ■ VALUES BASED STRATEGIC PLANNING: WHY PLAN?

CHAPTER 1 ■ WHO NEEDS TO PLAN?   3

Introduction   4
Schools as better places   7
Deficit thinking   9
Values and the people who make up schools   11
People, not results   12
A word about values   13
Big picture and chalk-face planning in schools   14
The leader's role   17
About this approach   17

CHAPTER 2 ■ STRATEGIC PLANNING   21

A fear of planning   21
Self-managing schools   24
Strategic planning as a system requirement   26
Strategic planning and school improvement   27
Strategic planning   30
Confronting the notion of strategic choice   31
Strategic planning in schools   39
Principles of effective strategic planning   41
Summary   49

CHAPTER 3 ■ STRATEGIC PLANNING AND ORGANISATIONAL REDESIGN   50

A fear of restructuring   51

Restructuring in schools 52
Reengineering in schools 55
Rethinking in schools 57
Summary 59

CHAPTER 4 ■ LEADERSHIP AND STRATEGIC PLANNING 61
The leader's role in strategic planning 62
Strategic planning and learning organisations 63
A school is a human invention 66
Strategic planning and the importance of people 68
Reframing: A way of elevating understanding 70
A new understanding of vision 73
Summary 77

CHAPTER 5 ■ STRATEGIC THINKING 78
Strategic thinking 80
The seven planning hexagons 81
Strategic management tasks versus critical
    operating tasks 85
Summary 95

CHAPTER 6 ■ VALUES 97
Values and educational administration 97
A cultural approach 99
Defining values 102
Values-driven schools 105
Traditional organisational values 107
Global issues: Whose values? 110
Top-down imposition of values to drive change 113
Shared values 114
Espoused values 116
What are values and how do they affect schools? 119
Values and student socialisation 122
School values and central requirements 126
Summary 130

CHAPTER 7 ■ COMPARING STRATEGIC PLANNING PROCESSES 131
Introduction 131
Traditional strategic planning processes 132
A committees approach 138

The values based strategic planning process   142
Differences between planning approaches   144

* * * * * * * * * * * * * * * *

SECTION 2 ■ VALUES BASED STRATEGIC PLANNING:
A PRACTICAL GUIDE

CHAPTER 8 ■ VALUES BASED STRATEGIC PLANNING   151
Introduction   151
How is planning carried out?   152
A summary of the steps in the values-based process   154

STEP 1 ■ INTRODUCTION   158

STEP 2 ■ VALUES SCAN   164
Writing value statements   165
Collating value statements   168
Towards one set of values   170

STEP 3 ■ CRITICAL ISSUES   174
Celebration point   177

STEP 4 ■ WRITING A MISSION STATEMENT   178

STEP 5 ■ KEEP, CHANGE AND TRY   183
Keep, change and try: As a client survey process   189

STEP 6 ■ COLLATING AND PRIORITISING KEY RESULT AREAS   190

STEP 7 ■ FOCUS SHEETS   193
Performance indicator writing   198

STEP 8 ■ PULLING IT TOGETHER   201

STEP 9 ■ CLIENT SCAN   205
In conclusion   212

* * * * * * * * * * * * * * * *

REFERENCES   215

INDEX   223

SECTION 1

Values Based Strategic Planning: Why Plan?

CHAPTER 1

Who needs to plan?

KEN asked a group of senior managers from schools, 'Do you believe in long-term planning?' The chorus 'Of course!' was accompanied by bemused looks. Ken then explained that the vast majority of such plans never come to fruition. 'Why do you continue to plan, then?' he asked. The answers amounted to the fact that people seek comfort from predicting the future, even if it is unpredictable!

Does this mean we should abandon the idea of planning altogether? No, we should not, but we should undertake a radical rethink about the way we tackle it. There seems to be little point in wasting hundreds of hours of professional time and effort on something that patently does not work.

If you are involved in school management and in planning any aspect of your school's work, or if you are a student of education management with a particular interest in institutional planning, this book is written for you. Whether you are responsible for formulating school improvement plans, development plans, action plans for improvement, corporate plans or any other form of plan, we believe that what we have to say is relevant, informative and important.

Most of the planning we are involved in is 'strategic' in nature. That means that you are supposed to identify the right 'strategies' for your school to be successful. Thus, our purpose here is to provide you with a step-by-step guide to strategic planning in schools. We shall also share with you the success we have had in developing strategic plans in many schools and other organisations across a number of countries. You are unlikely to find what we do in the standard textbooks on strategic management. We call our way of doing things 'values based strategic planning'.

Let us start the ball rolling with some fundamental questions. Try answering 'yes' or 'no' to each of these. Do you believe:

♦ that the purpose of planning in schools is to enhance the educational opportunities for students?

♦ that a school in Singapore is not the same as a school in the USA?

♦ that a plan is of no worth unless it affects people's actions?

♦ that people's actions are based on what they believe in?

♦ that people are not lazy or selfish, but will, if given the opportunity, contribute much to the school by voicing their opinions about what can be done, should be done and how the school can be more successful?

♦ that plans dreamt up by outsiders and handed down to teachers to adopt and implement are highly problematic?

♦ that collaboration means more than getting a draft of a paper for 'consultation'?

♦ that a person from outside your school who has never worked in your school (or education, for that matter) knows less about your school's success than the staff or parents of the school?

♦ that schools comprise people who are there to serve other people?

If you have answered 'yes' to most of these questions, then you are probably already with us in spirit and you may wish to move on to the second section of this book, where we explore how you can put the beliefs which are behind the questions into practice as you develop strategic plans for your school.

Introduction

■ The principal of St Andrew's Secondary School, Mrs Lim, decided at 4.21 p.m. on Tuesday, 23 September, that she hated

'Dr Death'. Mrs Lim was not really that sort of person, but in Dr James Chan's case, she felt her animosity was justified.

'Doc Death' was James Chan's nickname, a name given to him following his appearance at the school formal dinner on a motorbike wearing a biker's black leather jacket bearing the logo of a skull and crossbones. James Chan, 47, was highly regarded by staff and students alike. Not only did he have a PhD in science education (his thesis was on occupational health and safety), but he was a pretty good classroom teacher. He had chosen to remain in the classroom and had not attempted to scale the managerial career ladder. Outside school, he doted on his Harley-Davidson and read science history.

Mrs Lim reached the conclusion that she despised James Chan because, when she gave out the school's new school improvement plan, called 'St Andrew's in the 21st century', for staff comment, he openly and in front of the younger teaching staff declared it to be 'a ridiculous and blatant attempt by the school administration to single-mindedly put St Andrew's back into the educational dark ages'!

Of Mrs Lim, his comments were that the whole plan was clearly written by her on a 'wet Sunday after church when there was nothing else to do'. Stunned by the barrage of criticism, Mrs Lim thought of all the effort that had gone into working with the consultant from the ministry on the plan for over four months. She was more than offended.

This was the first time the teaching staff had seen the plan, but she had told them that it was only a draft. Besides, the consultant had distributed a questionnaire to all staff – of which less than 20 per cent had bothered to respond to – and they, the teachers, had been told that she had an 'open door'. Despite this, few had gone through it.

As far as Mrs Lim was concerned, James Chan was typical of the problem of schools in the 1990s: cynical, trendy teachers whose 'egos get in the way of proactive planning, and whose selfish concern for themselves interferes with the overall good of the school', to use her words.

Unfortunately for Mrs Lim, James Chan found strong support amongst most fellow teachers and many parents, and while she continued to push St Andrew's through towards the 21st century, she knew intuitively that the plan would end up on dusty shelves or in bottom drawers. ■

The principal's blueprint for success, so painstakingly developed and expertly written, had become the catalyst for a staff versus administration dingdong. Ironically, the plan, which should have united the school in a common vision for the future, had united teachers and the community against the school's executive.

This is not an isolated example. All too often, the release of a new strategic plan, a review or corporate plan by an education department, ministry or head office, or even by the school's management elite, leads to conflict and tension. Sometimes it goes further than the odd note of discontent voiced by the James Chans. For instance, in the state of Victoria in Australia, the release of the ministry's 1996 strategic plan to take education into the 21st century resulted in public street protests and strike action by tens of thousands of teachers.

Those in management who write the plans argue that they have to chart the future no matter how unpalatable it may be for some, and that conflict is inevitable because, as Kaufman (1992, p. 77) suggests, there is some sort of 'built in clash between proactive planning and many people's egos'. This is the belief that some – perhaps most – in management have: that people will always resist change and that it is in teachers' inherent nature to fight any plan, regardless of how good it is.

Have you heard that before? People resist change? It is true that plans may make life difficult for those in the organisation or community, but we disagree that conflict is inevitable, or that people naturally fight change. After all, do you think that a man suffering from the evils of starvation would resist a plan for ways to get food to him?

Beneath that pointed observation is a hint of the essence of change: that so much depends on how the change in our circumstances is seen and understood. We shall return to this issue in due course.

In this book, we will present from our many years of strategic planning experience in a number of countries a process of planning that is both realistic and open to account, yet which enables those most directly involved inside the organisation or in its community to feel a sense of ownership and commitment.

As we move into a new and promising century, planning in schools has taken on a new significance. With the expansion of self-managing schools, devolution of power and control, and increasing drives towards economic rationalism, and as schools around the world have been caught up in the push for greater accountability and for increasing demands for effectiveness, the need for schools to develop coherent plans of strategic intent has become more acute. Schools in many systems around the world are required to formulate strategic plans. Some are called school improvement plans, some action plans for school improvement, and yet others school development plans. Whatever the label, they all share the purpose of expressing ideas about where the school needs to be, what it should be achieving, and what it should be doing to achieve those ends. But planning needs to be more than this, for schools as service organisations need a planning process that enables them to define their identity, one that is based on how the people who make up the school and its community define success.

Our mission is to provide you with a practical and workable planning guide. We address our ideas to principals, like Mrs Lim, to school teachers and parents on school boards, and to students of education management. It is right that we mention members of school communities, since our way of approaching the problem of planning is one that draws communities together in a common understanding.

Schools as Better Places

Our book is about schools getting better. Call it 'school improvement' if you wish. It is about schools being better places for students and achieving improved educational outcomes. It is a guide to help you to:

- ◆ identify what your school exists to achieve;
- ◆ establish what the people who make up your school and the community it serves would define as success for your school;
- ◆ identify where your school should be, what it is, and how it can get better at what it does;
- ◆ set objectives that allow you to manage and deliver quality educational programmes;
- ◆ discover what it will take to make yours a more effective place of learning for students;

♦ develop concrete strategies and actions that are supported by staff;

♦ put into place plans that will enable you to evaluate your school's programmes for effectiveness, efficiency and appropriateness; and

♦ ensure that staff have no reason to become cynical or negative, or to be moved to resist innovation and change.

Try to think of what schools looked like ten or so years ago. If you have been in teaching for a while, you will not have to ponder too long to construct a picture which in many ways is different from what you see today. Many things, of course, remain the same (especially in classrooms), but if you focus on school governance, the shifts are considerable. Education is undergoing dramatic changes in conception, structure and expectation.

Now direct your thoughts to a process that has become a central feature of almost every school's consumption of time: planning. For most schools up to the mid-1980s, the only planning that principals had to be concerned about was that which necessitated returning standard forms to the department or ministry, deciding who would teach what to whom or getting programmes in on time. The only planning that teachers were concerned about was planning their class activities (programmes) or the odd sports carnival or other school event. Parental involvement in planning was usually limited to fund-raising activities or organising the local school centenary celebrations. Student involvement was unheard of. Most schools were simply not required to write plans, and few were familiar with the term 'strategic planning', that being thought of as something that applied only to the world of business and commerce.

Complex issues involving the school's future direction were, on the whole, the responsibility of senior educational professionals in central offices. Future priorities, curriculum, budget projections, staffing requirements, student demographics and policy changes were decided by district superintendents, inspectors, directors or other bureaucrats, and such processes rarely involved individual schools. Plans developed for schools were almost identical, whether the school was across the road from the central office or 2,000 kilometres away in an isolated rural area; or whether the school comprised mainly gifted children or those of lower educational attainment.

These days, however, it would be unusual for a school not to be involved in writing some form of business plan, development plan, strategic plan or action plan. Principals, teachers and parents are becoming increasingly responsible for the most complex and important aspects of the school's future, the strategic planning processes.

There are many ways of writing a school's strategic plan. One way would be for the principal and other members of the core elite to get together one weekend (over – or preferably after – a few drinks) and to deal with it just like they would the time-table or school budget. They would probably encounter as much success as Mrs Lim. What we intend to show you is how you can employ a meaningful approach to planning and how you can keep your weekends free for your own leisure.

If you see the responsibility for strategic planning as an opportunity to engage in a process of continuous improvement, you will gain from reading this book, because you will become more effective and efficient in what you do. Schools can no longer look to a distant bureaucracy to control their decisions. If they are willing to take it, they have new-found freedom to chart their own course, but to do this, they must take control of their own agendas and must plan what they want to happen.

We hope that you find this volume helpful as you seek to exert some control over your future and to lead your institution to higher planes of effectiveness in all that it is and does.

Deficit Thinking

Traditionally, strategic planning has most often been thought about in terms of a process that:

♦ describes where the organisation is going;

♦ sets the criteria for determining when you have arrived; and

♦ gives directions for making the right choices for actions and activities that will get you there.

Kaufman (1992, p. 5) says planning is a substitute for having to count on good luck. He believes that planning is about getting to where you need to be. He describes it as the process that enables an organisation to:

♦ identify where to go (and why);

♦ find exactly what should be accomplished to reach our chosen destination, and identify alternative ways and means for getting our required results and payoffs;

♦ select the best ways and means to get there;

♦ plan the design, development and implementation of those best ways and means; and

♦ evaluate how well we are doing and have done, and revise as required.

That seems all neat and tidy. Indeed, Kaufman (1992, p. 5) suggests that such an approach is 'simply rational'. But, if it is, why do so many organisations find that the result of such planning is far from satisfactory? While the plan itself may be well prepared and elegantly presented, its acceptability and implementation may be problematic. Perhaps there is a flaw in the process?

While Kaufman's stages of planning use the well-known travel saying – select a destination, figure out the best way of getting there, then explain how you know when you have arrived – underlying this process is a typically 'deficit' cognitive interest. Kaufman, like many others (we shall mention some of them later) views planning as a process of looking for deficits. It is the process of determining the 'gap' between what the organisation should be achieving (where it should be in terms of productivity, cost efficiency, and so forth) and what it is achieving. From this gap analysis, action plans can be made that will restructure or re-engineer the organisation to rectify this deficit. In other words, strategic planning has typically been about managers and leaders thinking that their organisations need to plan in order to rectify problems: to overcome production problems, to reduce costs, to get staff to work more effectively and with greater productivity, to take advantage of markets that have not been utilised, and so on.

The point we are making is that the deficit thinking which widely underpins traditional top-down strategic planning may be the very reason why planning, in so many situations, has been less than successful.

Values and the People Who Make Up Schools

Our view is that strategic planning should not be based on deficit thinking. What is missing from such thinking is the importance of people's values and deeply held beliefs. The place of people in the planning process is indeed of paramount importance.

That is not to say that traditional top-down strategic planning places no importance on people. Kaufman (1992), for example, argues that successful planning must have a humanistic dimension, that organisations' plans have to 'care for people'.

However, most strategic planning accounts for people as organisational resources – similar to financial and physical resources – that have to be used wisely. In accordance with such thinking, people become expendable and restructurable commodities and merely another aspect of the planning formula to be adjusted, directed and reviewed. Moreover, people, in traditional top-down planning, are often seen as having little knowledge or understanding of the 'big picture', of what the organisation needs to achieve. In schools, teachers, while valued for their contributions within the confines of their classrooms, are seldom valued for their strategic or corporate viewpoints.

Perhaps the human agents in our schools – the teachers and parents – should be seen in a different light: as people who are knowledgeable about their roles and about the 'structures' (such as the rules, accepted ways of doing things and historically developed procedures) of the schools of which they are a part. The role of strategic planning is to enable them to express themselves discursively. It is also its purpose to provide the environment, stimulus and opportunity which will enable these participants to be involved in intellectual, practical, ideological and moral critique.

This is indeed a lofty ideal. But strategic planning, we argue, is not about managers or leaders setting visionary targets and planning strategies for how best to *use* people to achieve such goals. Rather, strategic planning is about the organisation getting better at what it exists to achieve, and this cannot be done effectively without involving its people in a deep and meaningful way in planning its future.

People, Not Results

Strategic planning, as we have clearly stated, is about the school getting better at what it is there for. We have to guard, however, against the 'think results' colloqialism. Kaufman (1992, p. 12): 'So think *results* in order to define where to go to make sure that you get there'; and Kaufman and Herman (1991): 'In its most powerful use, strategic planning identifies results', are examples of traditional organisational thinkers who see strategic planning as very much results oriented.

Our view is that the results focus, particularly in service organisations such as schools, hotels, fire services and airlines, is both overly simplistic and highly problematic. A commitment to 'think results' may open up the risk of blinding ourselves to some of the most important factors impacting on success.

The 'think results' mentality stems from the motivational 'hype' of the 1970s, when organisations were seen predominantly as goal-oriented entities and little else. People were simply resources which could be manipulated or discarded. Of course, little has changed in some circles, except the language. Many still talk euphemistically about 'downsizing' and 'restructuring' as the logical responses to organisational failure. Replacing the chief with a new, perhaps more visionary, leader from outside may be part of the radical restructuring package. And if replacing people inside the organisation does not work, you could always try replacing the clients if they do not meet your market expectations!

Some of the more significant legislative and contractual developments that have taken place suggest that such thinking may be flawed. Enterprise bargaining, workplace agreements, natural justice legislation, laws against harassment and the promotion of gender equity are all signs that the single-minded pursuit of results as the basis of strategic planning is both anachronistic and possibly even hazardous.

We argue, like Greenfield (1980, p. 38), that the best way to underwrite planning is to resist thinking of organisations as goal-oriented systems, and to view them instead as social creations. In this light, then, schools do not control people but, rather, people control schools. This simple shift of thinking leads us to adopt that popular truism: organisations are about people.

Despite all this, schools should strive for excellence; they should pursue quality achievement vigorously and with determination; and they should aim to be the best they can be for their students and communities. This is very different, though, to saying they should be results oriented. Rather, they should be people oriented. From that conception, strategic planning is about charting how the people who make up a school – the staff, students, parents and certain other relevant people – can best work together to achieve the most worthwhile educational outcomes for the community they serve.

A Word about Values

Values based strategic planning suggests that planning is founded on values. Indeed, the very process must begin with values. Values anchor the operation of all service-oriented organisations, whether they are banks, airlines, government service agencies or schools.

The word 'values' conjures up for most of us the simple meaning of 'things we value'. That, in essence, is what we mean by values. But when we look at the concept more closely, we begin to understand its complexity and also its potential for the way we think and behave. Our attitudes, political preferences and religious beliefs all form part of a complex values fabric (Stott and Walker, 1995). Thus, values patterns in schools are powerful determinants of what happens in the principal's office and in the classroom.

Perhaps the easiest way to understand values in organisations is to ask the question, 'On what basis was that decision made?' All decisions made day to day or long term are anchored in the values of the organisation. The more deeply anchored they are, the more likely they are to become established norms. Some decisions that are made may be the 'wrong' decisions: they are counter to the values of the organisation or they result in outcomes that do not enable the organisation to achieve its purpose. Often, people may make decisions without being able to articulate their values or even the reasons for their decisions, but regardless of whether the values are conscious or subconscious, all decisions are anchored in them.

A school's values can best be described as:

> ■ The beliefs held by the people in an organisation about what their organisation is meant to achieve, and the principles that guide how they should act to achieve them. ■

Our approach to strategic planning is in line with Sergiovanni's broader conception of a values-based approach to school leadership. Sergiovanni (1995) states that the specification of beliefs and assumptions:

> ■ provides (schools) with a standard for determining what is good and bad, effective and ineffective, and acceptable and unacceptable. Using a values-based approach for defining the role of the principal not only ensures that what principals decide to do meets acceptable standards, but also provides the school with a set of indicators that defines its educational and moral health. (p. 7) ■

The same basic philosophy holds true for school-level strategic planning. Through clarifying shared values – what the school exists to achieve – schools prescribe *for themselves* acceptable standards and guides for decisions.

Big Picture and Chalk-face Planning in Schools

A useful book about strategic planning in schools needs to serve two purposes. The first is to provide a step-by-step process of strategic planning which covers the 'big picture'. In other words, the first purpose should be to provide a holistic view of the school, what the school as a whole entity exists to achieve, what the people (including staff and community) want of their school, and what the overarching goals, strategies, performance indicators and tasks are. Another name for this sort of global overview is 'corporate plan', implying an overall plan for the corporate entity.

The second purpose should be to provide guidance of utility to those who operate at the 'chalk face' (an appropriate metaphor for schools, surely). Some authors, like Kaufman (1992), would call this type of planning 'microplanning', in contrast to the big picture, which he would call 'macroplanning'.

We feel uncomfortable with these terms. While the expressions 'micro' and 'macro' have come widely into vogue, the former implies a smallness and insignificance, while the latter implies a grandness and importance. Kaufman (1992, p. 5) even suggests that there is a further stage in the scheme of things – 'megaplanning' – in which needs external to the organisation are addressed. In practice, we see limited difference in the magnitude of importance of these different levels.

Kaufman (1992, p. 5) states that it is very important to begin at the right level of planning and to proceed in the correct order. His is a traditional 'top-down' approach, as shown in Figure 1.1.

While such an approach may be reasonably applicable to some operations, for schools, especially mainstream schools within systems of education, such a top-down prescription of strategic planning may be flawed and highly problematic.

Figure 1.1 From Megaplanning to Consequences

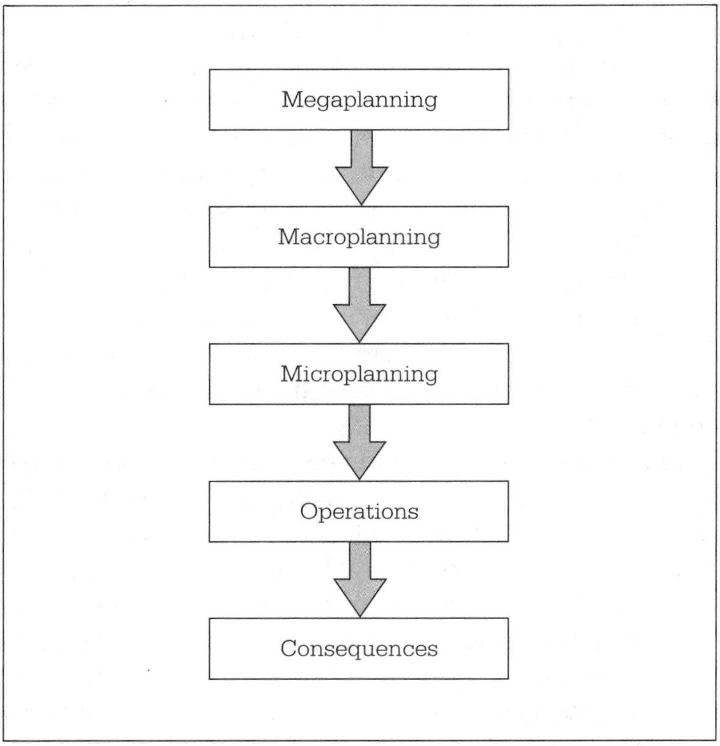

Bryson (1989, p. 47) describes Wayne Gretzky's (a world famous ice hockey player) micro-strategic thinking as 'I skate to where I think the puck will be'. For all of the megaplanning by ice hockey's managers and administrators, including patterns of attendance, sociological studies of the sport's impact on the community, federal funding and sponsorship; for all of the macroplanning by team coaches and managers – including game plans, motivational workshops, physical fitness training schedules, and teamwork building strategies – it all comes down to Gretzky skating to where he senses the puck will be! And Gretzky, as Bryson (1989) ironically notes, was not even given a pocket on his uniform in which he could carry a copy of the team's strategic plan!

There should be no differentiation between levels of planning: the so-called 'mega' is no more important than the 'macro', nor is the 'macro' more important than what people do at the operational level. Indeed, it seems to be at the 'chalk face' level that planning takes on its most meaningful form. Long-term, all-embracing plans lose their impact (if they ever had any) very soon after being written. As Stacey (1991) notes in *The Chaos Frontier*, such plans are seldom referred to because real events take over, progress against such plans is seldom monitored, the plans are out of date after six months, and the very process of matching existing resources to customer demands exposes organisations to more imaginative rivals. Strategic planning in successful operations appears to be handled differently to the way suggested in textbooks, and relies heavily on managers using implicit models to tackle current strategic issues. From this per-spective, there is probably more to support the need for short-term, localised strategic plans than there is to verify the utility of long-term expressions of intent.

If that seems to be an indictment of strategic planning, our criticism is for it as it appears in mainstream texts. We believe wholeheartedly in strategic thinking and in managing strategi-cally. It is a process, however, which applies to all those involved in the organisation, rather than merely to an elite band of senior executives. Teachers, for instance, must be able to step outside their classrooms to think strategically; similarly, parents must be able to articulate a wider concern than that which is just for their child's classes and education.

In this book, we provide concrete ways in which school leaders can help teachers and others – including parents and students – to think strategically. As part of a values-based approach to the process of planning, we advance a system of strategic thinking that includes 'seven planning hexagons', critical operating tasks and strategic management tasks. We also address the principle of critical success factors and the way in which they support strategic thinking.

The Leader's Role

Mrs Lim said:

■ | 'But you're missing the big picture, James. You cannot see beyond your classroom. I am telling you that the strategic plan I have written with the consultant is absolutely vital for this school's future'. ■

Mrs Lim, unbeknown to her and despite all her visionary leadership, is the one who has missed the picture. The great plan, no matter how insightful, will be as much use as yesterday's newspaper if her workforce, represented by James Chan in this case, is not able to think strategically – if it cannot 'skate to where the puck is'.

You may wonder what Mrs Lim's role is if, as the big chief, she cannot dream up plans which everyone should accept subserviently and with due deference. As a strong school leader, it is part of her remit, we would argue, to provide a structured and clearly understood path along which her professional colleagues can travel with her as the school develops its strategy. Her task is to guide her colleagues along this path, to provide the environment, stimulus and opportunity to enable them (and community members) to be involved in intellectual, practical, ideological and moral analysis of what the school should be doing, how it should be responding to client demands, what it needs to do to build its support in terms of enrolment, how it should be behaving, and what it should believe in.

About This Approach

Appropriately, we have structured this book on a values basis. It builds first from determining your values in terms of what your beliefs about strategic planning are and what it exists to achieve. Then we move on to examining how you might involve the people in your organisation in the process in order to achieve success.

A few moments ago, we outlined what Mrs Lim's role should be: that of providing a structured and clearly delineated path along which her colleagues could progress as they sought to develop a strategic agenda. Similarly, we shall guide you along a path, and we intend to provide the ideas, stimuli and opportunities to involve you in analysis of what the school should be doing as it plans its strategic intent. Such analysis entails an engagement with intellectual, practical, ideological and moral dimensions.

In Chapter 2, *Strategic Planning*, we open the way for you to think about your needs for planning and the choices you face in establishing effective plans for your school.

Chapter 3, *Strategic Planning and Organisational Redesign*, explores the link between the strategic planning process and the resulting changes that it brings about for the organisation. These changes, in some cases, may be relatively small; at other times, they may be so significant as to bring about major organisational redesign.

In Chapter 4, *Leadership and Strategic Planning*, we explore the nature and role of leadership in strategic planning. Strong leadership may be crucial to success, but that must not be confused with a rigidly hierarchical top-down approach, which is problematic when it comes to the formation of effective strategic plans. Strong leadership, as we conceptualise it in this process, means establishing a path – or framework, if you like – within which participants can be skilfully guided and accompanied.

Chapter 5, *Strategic Thinking*, explores strategic planning at the classroom level. We establish ways in which teachers, administrators and parents can develop strategic thinking skills. A strategic plan can have little impact unless those involved can think strategically. To assist in the process of developing strategic thinking skills, we explain several cognitive skills or tools, including seven planning hexagons, critical operating tasks, strategic management tasks and critical success factors.

In Chapter 6, *Values*, we discuss why our approach is called values based strategic planning. We pinpoint the differences between traditional top-down strategic planning processes that are based on scientific organisational thinking, and contrast these with the cultural perspective that a focus on values provokes. It is important for participants in the process to see the close link between values and making effective plans. We contest the belief that plans can be made outside the school. The proponents of such a process may explain the advantages of plans being 'values free', but plans can be of no worth unless they are about people's actions, what they do. And people's actions, are always informed by values. Similarly, copying plans and policy cloning – evident in many systems, from Hong Kong to Singapore and Australia – is a naïve process which, we argue, is doomed to failure in the longer term. Importing strategic policy and 'best practices' from the USA, from European countries and from Japan largely ignores the contextual imperatives in the home system, which in themselves are a complex amalgam of individual and societal values.

In Chapter 7, *Comparing Strategic Planning Processes*, we return to strategic planning at the school or system level. We describe two traditional strategic planning processes: a consultant-based top-down model; and a committee-based process. The latter is the most popular in schools, but it is a problematic and largely inappropriate model, as it fails to account for the key purpose which schools have of developing improved educational opportunities for children.

In the final chapter, *Values Based Strategic Planning*, we provide a thoroughly practical guide to values based strategic planning. The finer points of each part of the process are examined.

Schools are very different places today to what they were twenty years ago. That is due in part to the world in which we live. A host of factors, such as more informed, articulate and demanding parents; and significant – sometimes unpredictable – shifts in policy from central government, have had their effects on the way in which schools are managed and organised. In the contemporary context, 'adhocracy' is something we can ill afford, and planning, therefore, is important if schools are to fulfil their role and mission. Planning in itself, however, is of limited use unless it leads to the fulfilment of intent. That will not happen by executive imperative. What is needed is something that enables what we value, what we believe in and what we expect to be exposed and accounted for as we seek to influence and even determine our future. It is through such a process that we might enjoy the fruits of action and the joys of organisational success.

CHAPTER 2

Strategic planning

NOW we start to look at planning and, in particular, that form of planning which is intended to help the school exert some influence over its future. We shall look at a few of the significant events in school management which have raised the awareness of a need for planning, and we shall examine some of the purposes of planning institutional strategy. We shall define strategic planning and discuss some of the more important issues relating to the process of planning. This chapter also contains a note of caution: vision and mission formulation, goal setting and long-term planning are all likely to be meaningless exercises unless they are approached in the right way. We therefore point out some of the inadequacies of mainstream management practice as a warning to those who believe that prevailing practice will do the job.

A Fear of Planning

Here is a short story told by an ex-teacher about strategic planning in a department of education where she worked for over twenty-five years.

■ *The Ice Man Cometh*
I remember Iva Lopes well ... very well. It is like that with people who have had a major influence on your life. I remember so many details: his abrupt manner, his slightly tilted glasses, his occasional adolescent-like giggle. But most of all, I remember

him because twice, as a junior officer, he terrified the wits out of me.

Iva was a superintendent – the position below a divisional director and one level above a school principal – in our education department of over 3,800 teachers. He was unfortunate enough to be twice (admittedly, five years apart) taken off his normal duties as head of human resource management to conduct the department's strategic planning process, more usually known as 'the review'.

He was known by us as the Ice Man. The name bore no relation to his personality, but it accurately described his demeanour as chair of the strategic planning committee, known to teachers as the 'razor gang'.

I remember Iva because he made 'change' and 'planning' words to be feared; if there was any potential for challenge or excitement in them, he removed such benefits. Iva separated his personal beliefs from his professional actions: 'I am doing this because it is what I am paid for. You don't think I actually enjoy it, do you?'

He probably didn't, but he did not share the grief. He did most things on his own. Iva spent about six months on a plan, starting with a mission statement (usually authored by the chief executive officer) followed by a comprehensive audit and a survey of client needs. From the information, he would recommend organisational restructuring, which would inevitably include job losses, which he, euphemistically, called 'downsizing'. Fear, suspicion and even hate abounded as jobs were put in jeopardy and offices were relocated.

The signs of impending doom were uncannily consistent. A change in the official letterhead usually signalled the new strategic plan's implementation, and the department's phone directory became of little use, except as an ergonomic device for propping up computers! As far as teachers were concerned, Iva's reviews had little impact on the education of children. The teachers' reaction was to close their classroom doors tight and carry on as normal. Fancy logos, as far as they were concerned, changed nothing in the classroom.

There was some impact, though. The department achieved a higher level of efficiency, and the restructuring led to cost benefits. It didn't really matter what was being done so long as it was done well. Doing things right was the order of the day, and it worked. Of course, there were no improvements in teaching and learning. Quite the reverse, in fact. Iva's efforts usually led to teacher griping, and I am sure there were losses in effectiveness. After all, how can people work productively when someone is doing his best to make them miserable? And what about the effects on children of being taught by demoralised teachers? ∎

Iva saw his job in the strategic planning process as both necessary and impersonal. He was a creature of his times. He saw what he did as a way of improving the system's effectiveness and cost efficiency. He had scant regard for people and their values. He was not alone in this view. He was the product of an age when management theorists developed models of organisations as soulless entities. Accordingly, he could – or so he thought – do as he liked, since he had the power of position, and people would have to comply.

Not an unfamiliar scenario. In this chapter we challenge such conceptions of planning, where everything stems from the top and, supposedly, those at the bottom behave in obedient compliance; where, in linear fashion, plans lead to determined outcomes. We challenge apparently values-free approaches to planning, such as practised by Iva Lopes.

Strategic planning is becoming an increasingly common strategy for driving school change. Although our purpose is not to enter into a detailed description of the range of reforms being encountered in many systems, we give some attention to several movements which have had a significant effect on the way in which schools are managed. These movements include self-managing schools, school improvement, restructuring, and the learning organisation concept. Linked to such developments is an increasing recognition of the role of teaching staff in ensuring successful change, and a new understanding of the leader's role in strategic planning. When taken together, these developments provide useful guidance on both change and the ways it might be successfully managed. We start by looking at two significant movements – self-managing schools, and school improvement – and seek to explain how these have led to the need to engage in the planning of institutional strategy.

Self-managing Schools

Amongst a proliferation of school reforms throughout the world during the 1980s and 1990s, arguably the most dominant feature has been that of a pressure to move towards school-based management. The decentralisation movement has affected educators, to varying degrees, in Australia, the UK, Canada, New Zealand, Hong Kong, Singapore and some parts of China and the USA. In fact, it is fair to say that most systems throughout the world have been influenced, at least to some degree, by moves towards decentralisation (Dimmock and Walker, 1997). The trend has been reinforced by political ideologies and has mirrored such policy imperatives as privatisation – in some cases, on an unprecedented scale.

In England and Wales, the Conservative government, which was in power until 1997, vigorously pursued a policy of expanding the grant-maintained sector – a form of self-management – and supported the move by making it financially advantageous for schools to opt out of local authority control. Even the new Labour government, which many thought would be opposed ideologically to the grant-maintained concept, showed no inclination to dismantle it. This is not surprising in view of the fact that the prime minister sent his child to a grant-maintained school! In Hong Kong, strengthening moves towards self-managing schools were promoted by Education Commission Report Number 7 (Education Commission, 1996). Framed by a desire to improve the quality of school education, the commission recommended 'that all schools should by the year 2000 practise school-based management in the spirit of the School Management Initiative so that they can develop quality education according to the needs of their students'.

In Singapore, moves towards greater school autonomy began in earnest in 1987 in the report 'Towards Excellence in Education' (Ministry of Education, 1987). Amongst the report's major recommendations was a call for more school-based control. The report stated: 'Greater authority should be given to principals and teachers to enable them to develop appropriate educational programmes for pupils under their charge' (p. 75). While developments have taken root progressively since then, there has been a greater call in recent times for accelerating the process of decentralisation. The 'cluster' concept – whereby a small group of schools is looked after by a senior principal – is evidence of a commitment to devolving increasing levels of power to institutions. In Australia, Caldwell and Spinks (1988, 1992) argue that the move towards school autonomy is now so widespread that it merits being called a 'megatrend'.

Autonomy can take many shapes and forms, but Caldwell and Spinks (1992) help by providing a useful definition of the self-managing school. It is:

> ■ a school in a system of education where there has been significant and consistent decentralisation to the school level of authority to make decisions related to the allocation of resources … the school remains accountable to a central authority for the manner in which the resources are allocated. (p. 4) ■

The movement has by no means been implemented smoothly and has been criticised extensively on many fronts. Smyth (1993), questioning the stated purposes for moves towards devolution, outlines some of these criticisms:

♦ It is a way of the state arrogantly shirking its social responsibility for providing an equitable education for all.

♦ It treats schools as if they were convenience stores, and it deflects attention from national issues by making people in schools into managers and entrepreneurs. (p. 8)

Smyth's views are not shared by Caldwell (1994), who sees school-based management as an opportunity to transform education for the better. That may well be an opinion affirmed by schools in the UK, which have enjoyed an increase in the resources at their disposal after years of frustration in dealing with the stranglehold of local authority bureaucracy.

Whatever one's views, self-management is a fact of contemporary educational life and there is nothing to suggest any imminent change. As Caldwell (1994) notes:

> ■ In general, school-based management has been received well by school communities, despite opposition and scepticism at the outset and shortcomings in implementation along the way.

> Any reading of opinion suggests that the overwhelming majority of schools in the nations mentioned would not wish to return to more centralised arrangements. (p. 77) ■

The continued success of self-managing arrangements, we would argue, hinges to a large extent on the fundamental process of strategic planning. As O'Donoghue and Dimmock (1996) suggest:

> ■ The philosophy underpinning 'self-managing schools' is grounded in a planning process, the basis of which involves participative goal setting by stakeholders who form the school community. (p. 74) ■

The growing importance of school-based planning for growth and change has been instigated in large part by the autonomy movement. Previously, schools had little need to develop strategic plans, since this was a process that was the preserve of central authorities. Now, it has become essential, if not mandatory.

Strategic Planning as a System Requirement

The importance placed on strategic planning in recent years has been apparent across systems and countries (O'Donoghue and Dimmock, 1996). Different forms of strategic planning – school growth plans, school improvement plans, school action plans and school development plans – are commonplace in many systems, including Australia, the UK (see Edinborough, 1994), the USA, Singapore and Hong Kong.

Since 1991, schools in Hong Kong that have joined the School Management Initiative (SMI) have been required to develop Annual School Plans. By the turn of the century, all schools in the Special Administrative Region (SAR) will be required to engage in development or strategic planning as a key strategy for improving overall school quality. The Department of Education (DOE) guidelines describe the requirement for SMI schools thus:

> ■ The annual school plan is the outcome of the process of enabling those connected with the school to plan its management structures; to establish priorities in education, management and resources; and to develop systems of monitoring, evaluation

and review. Experience and systematic studies have shown that the process of producing a plan is as important as the product itself. Moreover an annual school plan drafted in collaboration with school staff results in greater commitment to the plan by all involved. (DOE, 1992, p. 1) ■

Similarly, schools in Singapore as part of their operation and school appraisal must develop school work plans. These comprise a three-year (strategic) rolling plan and a detailed annual work plan. The underlying philosophy of the need to plan was expressed in the influential report 'Towards Excellence in Education' (Ministry of Education, 1987), which stated:

■ It is imperative that a school establish its purpose, formulate its policy and objectives and chart its course … An effective organisation invariably is one that sets about its task with a clear vision of its role, identifies what it would like to achieve and brings wisdom to bear in the choice of its approaches. To ensure some certainty of success, to begin with, any school must decide what it would like to make of itself and so justify its existence. (p. 11) ■

All Australian state and territory education systems have also implemented strategic planning requirements (Davies, Weller and Lewis, 1989, cited in Cutterance, 1995) as a means of addressing new policies (Cutterance, 1995). Such planning is seen as a key component of the 'Schools of the Future' policy initiative in the state of Victoria. All schools in Victoria must develop a school charter in which the emphasis is placed on planned, coherent and continuous improvement. To quote from the document:

■ A quality charter provides a philosophical and operational framework for each school in the government schooling system. Schools will develop charters that reflect both the educational needs of their communities and the policies and priorities of government. (p. 2) ■

Strategic Planning and School Improvement

As we can see, strategic planning is a requirement of schools in at least several countries' educational systems. But it is more than a 'requirement of government'. Planning is now widespread at the school level as a means of better coping with development and change. It is considered a key platform for school improvement. (For a good summary of school improvement efforts worldwide, including Hong Kong, mainland China and Taiwan, see Cheng, 1995.) This leads us to the second significant movement that we look at in this chapter: the school improvement movement. The International School Improvement Project (ISIP) provides us with one definition of school improvement (Glatter, 1988). It is:

> ■ a systematic, sustained effort aimed at change in learning and other related internal conditions in one or more schools, with the ultimate aim of accomplishing educational goals more effectively. (p. 125) ■

Mortimore (1996a) provides a more recent explanation. School improvement, he states, is:

> ■ a generic term for a range of activities involving change. It is based on the application of school effectiveness findings. It focuses on both schools and pupils. It seeks to improve learning opportunities and to raise standards of achievement. (p. 5) ■

The general underlying philosophy of the school improvement movement 'is that the process is in the hands of the school itself. Thus, the principal, staff and school community have the power to decide what to do' (Mortimore, 1996b, p. 259). As we have already said, a key facet of school improvement is a commitment to strategic planning. The two – improvement and planning – appear to be inextricably linked. Hargreaves and Hopkins (1991), for instance, suggest that the purpose of development planning is to improve the quality of teaching and learning of a school through the successful management and innovation of change. Stoll (1992) too notes that school strategic plans (she calls them 'school growth plans') are a worldwide phenomenon and are clearly related to the almost universal school improvement movement.

School improvement depends primarily on schools engaging collaboratively in systematic planning processes that must ultimately lead to improved student outcomes. The plan's importance is seen as providing both a process and a clear indication of the way in which the school as an organisation intends to grow and change. Stoll (1992) believes that, as a part of the school improvement process, strategic plans should be derived from a sequential collaborative process, should include a vision of the future and should incorporate goal setting for a three-year period. For her, school planning needs to comprise:

- ◆ an assessment of the current state of the school and student outcomes;
- ◆ an identification of priorities and a plan of action;
- ◆ details about the plan's implementation; and
- ◆ a reassessment of outcomes and an evaluation of the plan to see if it has made a positive difference. (p. 114)

Strategic plans focus on a school's strong points. Improvement in this sense is concerned with building on strength. The starting point is normally a profile, audit or snapshot of the school's situation – a picture of the existing characteristics that make it effective and that can be built on as a part of the process of school improvement. In particular, it is important to assess:

- ◆ values: what the staff and the school's community are committed to;
- ◆ key result areas: what the school does that achieves its best results in enhancing student learning and in developing worthy citizens; and
- ◆ regional, system or community initiatives and expectations that are likely to impact on the school's work (environmental scan).

Once such an assessment has been carried out, the school needs to be involved in a collaborative process of identifying the most important areas for attention, and, using these as a base, needs to develop a plan of its priorities. Collaboration must not be confused with consensus. It is more about working together than about agreement. What is sought at this stage is for as many stakeholders as possible to be involved in the decision process. Stakeholders might include parents, students, non-teaching assistants, all teachers and administrators.

That is just a brief outline of the essence of strategic planning. As we claimed earlier, it is a clear and coherent response to calls for school improvement. Seen in that light, planning is essential. Flexibility in terms of the institution and its personnel, responsiveness to change, and building on the school's identified strengths are all features that might accrue from effective planning.

Strategic Planning

Strategic planning has been a feature of profit-making organisations for a long time, but it is only in recent years that longer term planning has become evident in schools. Whereas in the past schools were able to receive directions from central sources and plan operationally, they are now in the position of considering their futures and trying to influence them.

Planning has featured prominently in the general management literature for the past few decades at least. Strategic planning in particular has received considerable attention. Mintzberg (1994), however, claims that the concept of planning is often confused with general terms such as decision making and management and suggests that the most accurate and appropriate definition of planning should be:

■ a formalised procedure to produce an articulated result in the form of an integrated system of decisions. (p. 12) ■

Other definitions of strategic planning equate the process with positioning the organisation so that future prospects can be maximised and future risks minimised. In other words, strategic planning is about making choices concerning possible positions organisations may find themselves in and then evaluating the options so that the most desirable course of action is selected.

Such definitions are somewhat more accessible than the more typical one provided by Chantico Technical Management (1989), which defines strategic planning as:

■ the process of deciding on the objectives of the organization, on change in these objectives, on the resources used to attain these objectives, and on the policies that are given the acquisition, use, and disposition of these resources. Strategic planning is a process having to do with the formulation of strategic plans and policies that determine to change the character or direction of the organization. (p. 3) ∎

Kaufman (1992), in a less obscure variation, defines strategic planning as follows:

∎ It begins by identifying what should be and what could be. It then works to ensure that all of an organisation's parts are properly designed and focused. The first step is to define the results and payoffs that the organisation and each of its parts must contribute. It provides the missing ingredients for your organisation's survival, success, and meaningful social contribution. (p. ix) ∎

Strategic planning is reported widely as being essential for all organisations as they encounter change. While the literature suggests that there are at least nine schools of thought on strategic planning, almost all have been developed for use in the private sector and some have found their way into educational institutions. While these schools of thought contain different emphases, the basis is essentially the same: they are largely variations of a top-down approach that places senior management at the centre of the planning process.

It is not our intention in this chapter to debate the relative merits of different emphases in strategic planning, but it is useful to be aware that different foci exist within a seemingly unitary concept. A good source for understanding the intricacies of 'modern' strategic planning is Mintzberg's (1994) *The Rise and Fall of Strategic Planning*. A good historical perspective of the various schools of thought underpinning strategic planning is provided by Bryson (1989). We have summarised Bryson's synthesis in Table 2.1. In Chapter 7, we compare such models with the values-based approach.

Confronting the Notion of Strategic Choice

While it would be simple enough to accept the need to influence the organisation's future in some way through trying to dictate what should or will happen, we must first explain our views on

Table 2.1   Schools of Thought on Strategic Planning

School of Thought	Authors
Harvard policy model	Andrews, 1980; Christenson et al., 1983
Strategic planning systems	Lorange, 1980; Lorange et al., 1986
Stakeholder management approaches	Freeman, 1984
Content approaches Portfolio methods	Henderson, 1979; Wind and Mahajan, 1981; MacMillian, 1983
Competitive analysis	Porter, 1980, 1985; Harrigan, 1981
Strategic issues management	Ansoff, 1980; King, 1982; Pflaum and Delmont, 1987
Strategic negotiations	Pettigrew, 1977; Mintzberg and Waters, 1985
Logical Incrementalism	Quinn, 1980; Lindblom, 1959
Framework for Innovation	Taylor, 1984; Pinchot, 1985

Source: Bryson (1989, p. 24).

strategic choice. If you were to ask school principals what they should do to ensure the successful future of their schools – we do this all the time in our work, although our questions may be phrased differently – they would tell you several things, and there is a remarkable consistency of answer, regardless of which educational system they operate in.

First, they would say you must have a vision. When they use that word, they do not all mean the same thing. Some think of visions as dreams of what the organisation could look like if someone were to wave a magic wand, while others use the expressions 'vision' and 'mission' synonymously. Vision to them is what the school should be seeking to achieve. Then they would tell you that you must have goals or targets which are attainable, and if you meet these shorter term objectives, you are more likely to achieve the longer term mission. These statements – you will find them plastered over school walls in some systems like Singapore's – are meant to be relatively permanent and are usually sufficiently vague to make anything the school does acceptable. Some have an element of focus – like 'this school seeks to achieve the highest academic standards' – while others can be described as relatively ambitious – 'our school seeks to make the world a finer place to live'. More specifically, principals will tell you that you must analyse the school and its performance, and then, through a clever vault of mind, you will know what to do.

Second, principals will tell you that, once having decided on a vision, you must get everyone committed to it. In other words, you must be persuasive enough to cajole people into accepting your ideas. Because things do not quite work out so neatly, they will establish team building activities – so that 'we can all gel together and pull in the same direction' – and culture change programmes. We all know that this is not easy, but there is much advice in contemporary literature on how to disturb the status quo and to persuade people that change is not such a bad idea.

Third, principals will tell you that everything must be written down in the form of a plan of action. This sets out what must be done, by whom, when and possibly how. The whole idea of this process is to capture the spirit of what customers want and to match their requirements to what is provided.

Ken was talking recently to his former primary school head-teacher, who commented on 'all this nonsense' about planning. In his day, he pointed out, principals and teachers just got on and did things in the best interests of the children. Yet, present day school leaders articulate the planning model outlined above with consummate ease and a degree of commitment. How things have changed. The influence of principalship training programmes and in-service management development programmes has been pervasive.

We are not convinced, however, that this widely practised approach actually works as a way of controlling the school's future. It may sound good, but do principals and their senior colleagues actually work in such an explicit way when the next six months are not exactly predictable?

We have already alluded to the problems with mission state-ments and the like. As Stott and Walker (1992) pointed out in their research into mission statements in Singaporean schools, such statements tend to be alike. In fact, so bland and similar are they that they are instantly forgettable. Yet, we are told that uniqueness is an attribute and that schools should be dwelling on their differences. Some may argue that schools are all concerned with the same overarching purpose, but conversations with principals lead you to a different conclusion. Difference does exist, but it is not expressed.

Still on the subject of visions and missions, we do not believe that even a semipermanent view of what the school should be like at some point in the future is a recipe for success. Rather, like Stacey (1991), we see the importance of addressing a number of issues, opportunities, problems and challenges, and exploring them. Some of them should become more prominent on the agenda, some should be dropped, and some should be acted on even though they might well lead to failure. This is what actually happens, we suggest. The real world is more messy than the tidy world of missions, plans, goals and all the rest, as important as they have become.

At this point, we must mention a word that will appear frequently – 'difference'. We cannot accept the widely held belief in common values and shared beliefs. A successful future is more likely to emerge, we contend, from differences – differences in values, views, opinions – and the overemphasis on consensus building is likely to be counterproductive, since change, innovation and doing new things rely more on difference than on 'sameness'.

Now, let us move on to strategic plans and raise some questions about their usefulness. First, long-range plans are invariably influenced by a model which devotes attention to lists of strengths, weaknesses, opportunities and threats. The process of going through these may actually be useful, but people are seldom clear about what they should do once they have generated the list. When these are coupled with copious resource and financial projections, they are difficult to take seriously, because projections are merely guesses, and guesses are wrong more often than not.

Long-range plans (or strategic plans – it does not matter at this stage what you choose to call them) are often filed away and forgotten. When important issues come onto the agenda – like the one about the First Steps Programme which Mrs Lim had to encounter (we will tell you about that a little later) – the plan is seldom referred to. That is because the issue was not in the plan!

One of our more important observations is this: long-term plans are out of date within six months. Some would argue they are out of date as soon as they are written, and there is an element of truth in that, since unpredictable things happen daily. If the school has been doing the right things, they should bear little resemblance to what was written in a plan at least several years ago.

We have said it already, but it is worth repeating: planning strategically is a messy business. Taking conflicting opinions, accommodating changing circumstances and making difficult choices from amongst a range of alternatives are all problematic. Unfortunately, the world does not work like the 'expert' planner would have us believe. There is no evidence – in schools at any rate – of a linear relationship between intent and outcome. In other words, if we plan something today, it does not mean that it will happen on schedule tomorrow. Indeed, the relationship between what is intended and what actually happens is anything but linear.

Our final point in relation to the problems with long-term planning is that it tends to be based on history and parallel: it uses past experience and the knowledge of what other organisations may be doing as the guides to choice. That leads therefore to imitation and makes the school vulnerable to more imaginative institutions, especially if it sees them in a competitive light (Stacey, 1991).

All this leads us to suggest that there is a paradox between what principals and their senior colleagues espouse and what they actually do in times of uncertainty and change. It is clear that models of visions, missions and long-range plans are not working and that managers do something different. This does not mean that we abandon the notion of planning as a worthwhile activity, but rather that we account for what managers really do and for the reality of schools as organisations in writing any prescription for influencing the future. That is precisely what we have done in our model. In order to understand what is really going on, we need to ask two important questions: first, if we know that existing planning models do not work, why do people still continue to devote considerable time and energy to them? and, second, how do administrators in schools really control and develop their institutions?

Despite what strategic management writers would have us believe, the future is not knowable, and that applies to schools as much as it does to commercial organisations. Yet, they assume that it is less than problematic to formulate visions and missions. The explanation for the unknowability is that everything is linked to everything else. Schools, parts of schools, the education system, the economy and a range of other things are all connected. A seemingly insignificant change in one can lead to radical changes in other parts of the wider system. A minor economic episode in one country can lead to a major curriculum change in another country's secondary schools. That is not an isolated example, and you can probably think of your own instances in which unforeseen impacts have occurred.

If visions and plans do not work, why do administrators stick with them? The first reason is a compelling one: the discussion process itself may lead to key issues being brought into the arena. Of course, that assumes that people are given the opportunity to participate in the debate, and we shall be addressing this point later in the chapter.

Another reason may be that long-term planning (with the accompanying paraphernalia of visions and missions) emphasises the importance of thinking strategically, as opposed to reacting to short-term events. Thus, it sends a signal to organisational members that considering the school's future is an important process.

Perhaps the most intriguing reason is that long-term planning provides a false sense of security. It relieves the anxiety that is provoked by not knowing what tomorrow will bring. Of course, we still do not know what will happen tomorrow, but planning provides a useful palliative.

We doubt whether these are very good reasons for continuing with something which is less than effective. Even the desire to raise the issues through discussion is questionable. Would it not be more profitable to employ a process which devotes its attention to improving the quality with which strategic issues are handled? Surely, a higher level of capability in dealing with the issues that count would reduce the anxiety levels – if that is a good thing anyway?

We advocate Stacey's (1991) approach to strategy, and there is a parallel between what he calls 'strategic issue agendas' and our references to 'key issues'. The issues are those problems, opportunities and challenges which have wide and longer term consequences for the school. The agenda is dynamic. It is constantly changing – an important feature, for us, of effective strategic planning – and some items disappear, while new ones emerge.

The emphasis is on 'now' and not on the future. This may sound paradoxical in the light of our discussion on future strategy formulation, but we argue that thinking strategically is not about intending to do something tomorrow but rather doing something *now* to deal with things which will have an impact on tomorrow. Some may call that proactivity.

How we select issues for attention is a matter worthy of our consideration. By nature, we are ordered people. We seek order and logical explanations in things. But whatever we observe is subject to our frames of reference. Our beliefs, assumptions and values guide the way we look at what happens. To complicate matters, our basic assumptions are below the awareness level and we thus find them difficult to question. For example, if one of our key issues is poor performance in mathematics by some pupils, our basic, almost unchallengeable assumptions may be that the students are not receiving instruction or that they are just lazy. Our response may be to set up remedial classes so that they can get more of the same thing. The basic assumption here could be that the more you do something, the better you would be at it. The assumption may, of course, be true. And then again, it may not. What if the poor performance is really due to an in-compatibility between certain students' learning styles and the teacher's approach to instruction?

The next assumption is more serious. It is the belief that in a fast-changing environment we can exert effective control over what happens. We cannot do this, and there are many examples from the world of economics which suggest that control is an absurd concept in the context of a global economy. Just as mis-placed is the belief that those at the top of our schools – principals and other senior administrators – can exert tight control over the school's direction. Our typical behaviour in difficult times is to look upwards and to expect those 'up there' to know what to do. We also believe that, when things go wrong, there must be a clear cause. This is natural, but it stems from a belief that everything can be explained. If every effect had a clear cause, the world would be immensely more predictable. We would indeed be able to impose a degree of order. But the social world is not akin to the scientific world of supposed objectivity and certainty.

The point we are making here is that much of what we use for planning in schools (and other organisations, for that matter) has its root in a tradition which is far removed from the reality of our chaotic and dynamic contemporary world of education. If the words which best describe our context are uncertainty, unpredictability, irregularity and discontinuity, how can we employ planning models which are designed specifically for those words' antonyms? It seems bizarre that we try to plan for a world that simply does not exist. If our notions of strategic control are an illusion, what we need is a way of having some impact on our future, one that is characterised by those very words shown above. In the pages which follow, it is our task to provide a model which accounts for those conditions.

Despite the levels of unpredictability and uncertainty, we can make an impact on our organisations. There are things we can do to 'intervene'. We can give our schools a little 'push'. Morgan (1997) gives some examples of actions and events which can move the organisation along:

> ■ Experiments, prototypes, changes in rewards, changes in key personnel, a fiscal crisis, staff lay-offs and numerous other events, actions and experiences can themselves embody powerful messages that catalyse other changes in the context as the system adjusts itself to the new reality. (p. 270) ■

What we cannot do is to determine the outcomes of those changes. But the point made is an important one. Selecting the right things to do at the right time is a key strategic decision. These are what Morgan (1997, p. 271) calls the 'double high leverage initiatives'. Small changes and interventions can have an impact out of all proportion to their scale. 'A person wishing to change the context in which they are operating should search for "double" high leverage initiatives that can trigger a transition from one attractor to another'.

As Morgan goes on to say, in complex, non-linear systems, even seemingly minor changes can produce large-scale, significant effects. 'If people focus on finding high leverage initiatives within their spheres of influence that have the capacity to shift the context, potentials for major change can be unleashed' (p. 272). The small changes in themselves may be so pivotal that they lead to a major effect, or, together, they combine to produce a significant force.

Strategic Planning in Schools

There is a danger admittedly that we would abandon strategic planning as a hopeless quest in an uncertain world. This is not the case. We see it as a vital activity to any school, but it needs to be addressed within the context of what we have described above. Much depends on what we do here and now; how we ensure that the critical issues are brought onto the agenda (such critical issues may be thought of as the 'high leverage intiatives'); and how we make certain that people are involved to the extent that they can combine to form strong support units around those issues. Making them strong implies an element of political skill. Morgan (1997, p. 271) seems to confirm that view in suggesting that by 'getting key opinion leaders behind the initiative, he or she may be able to create the crucial time or space in which success can be demonstrated, publicized and made irreversible'.

An example of this comes from the university sector:

> ■ Sitting in a meeting with officers from the ministry and several university representatives including the dean, Paul, an ordinary lecturer, picked up from a conversation that the ministry people were keen for teachers taking in-service courses to get some form of recognition, like a certificate. The word 'accreditation' was mentioned. Paul pricked up his ears, as he had gained much experience in accreditation from his previous job. After the meeting, he mentioned to the dean how he would like to produce a paper outlining some ideas about how teachers could gain recognition. He spoke to a couple of the ministry officers to gain support. He then worked with an administrator and the

> person in charge of in-service courses to produce a paper. He saw an accreditation process as having great potential, and he formed a politically strong interest group round the issue. The dean was also attracted, because it was a means of gaining more support for courses and for leading people onto further award programmes. ■

There are several important points to note in this short case. Paul won support because he gathered some key people together. He also made sure accreditation was on the agenda, because he regularly kept the dean informed and kept contact with ministry officers, who in turn asked about progress regularly. Note too that the group *did* something which could influence what happened in the future: the members of the group produced a document and spoke to people. Of course, the next stage was to plan what would happen. This was an important strategic issue for the university, for it raised the possibility of significant income generation as well as providing more attractive educational opportunities for serving teachers.

We see strategic planning in schools as being primarily concerned with improving educational outcomes for students. Planning, beyond what we can do here and now, is the process of determining how decisions will be made that inform the actions of the staff and community, which will in turn lead to school improvement. Like Kaufman (1992, p. ix), we suggest that planning should be about *what should be* and *what could be*, which we define as what the school *values*. Unlike Kaufman, we believe that organisations like schools do not exist independently of the people who work in them or use their services. Planning, from our perspective, must be a shared task amongst all the people concerned with the school, for it is only when staff, parents and students think strategically that strategic plans can be of any use in improving educational opportunities. Strategic plans must thus allow all people in the school to see what role they can play in helping to achieve what it values.

But even that statement is misleading. It is the people involved who value things, not the school. In fact, the principal's view on what should be valued is usually expressed as 'what the school values'. What we were advocating earlier, therefore, was the scope for people to gather around issues which they value.

Taken together, these issues can be construed as what 'the school' values. This, as you will see later, is the essence of our values-based scheme.

Strategic planning, to us, is simply about positioning yourself and doing things to take advantage of your situation. It is best understood as defining the uniqueness of your school and the role it fulfils within its environment. Consequently, a strategic plan should be founded on the school's uniqueness and its role: what should be done and what could be done. This means beginning with an understanding of what the people who work in or use the organisation value. Values can be defined simply as what people *believe* the organisation should be doing. We shall explore this issue in depth and in a practical way in Chapter 8.

Strategic plans should be flexible, adaptable to changing circumstances, and relatively simple to develop and implement. They have a dual purpose. They are developed to *achieve* organisational values, and at the same time are developed *from* organisational values.

A strategic plan is not an unchallengeable edict that sets for all time (or for three years anyway) the school's direction and programmes. The document itself is merely evidence that something has happened: that the school has considered what it should and could do within the context of the beliefs and values of those who are part of it.

Putting strategic plans into place involves establishing a cultural process for participative change and involves considering the cultural and political realities of the organisation. For schools to survive in today's environment of dynamic complexity, it seems essential that they have at least some say in what they are going to do. They must attempt to control their destiny to some extent. Strategic planning helps schools to achieve this by targeting the constantly shifting environment and by placing a heavy emphasis on culture, reality and effectiveness.

Principles of Effective Strategic Planning

Let us pause here a moment to check out the argument so far. Strategic planning is seen as a linchpin for school improvement, but this does not mean that it is necessarily well done or has achieved its desired effect. A landmark study by MacGilchrist et al. (1995, cited in Mortimore, 1996b) found that planning was often very poorly done. Mortimore's summary identifies some of the common problems which we shall address as we move through the book:

> Our data show that, although developmental planning for improvement is being undertaken and is absorbing a great deal of time and energy, in only a minority of cases is it fully successful; i.e., the plan is what we term *corporate*. By this we mean that it involves the full staff, is co-ordinated with all other planning issues in the school, and that it impacts positively on learning in the classroom. We have characterised the development plans in other schools as *rhetorical* (mainly fine words), as *singular* (where they appear to be the property of the principal) or as *cooperative* (where they have some properties of the corporate plan but have not yet reached the classroom). (p. 261, emphasis in original) ■

Mortimore goes on to describe some of the challenges he sees for improving schools:

> You can start by making sure your school has an appropriate mission. This means thinking hard about the clients you serve and the needs they have, the resources you can offer, and the future demands of your community and society ... Creating a mission or reinventing an existing one will necessitate working closely with parents and the school community. (p. 261) ■

Mortimore raises an important issue in relation to mission: it has to be collaboratively formulated if it is to serve its purpose. Stott and Walker (1992) made that very point in their research into mission in Singaporean schools, where mission was clearly stated but no one knew what it was! It had become the rhetoric of school walls and prospectuses, but no one 'lived' it because they had had no part to play in inventing it. We shall address this and other issues as we describe in the pages which follow our experience of operating *values based strategic planning*.

While strategic planning is seen as a key component of self-managing schools and the school improvement movement, there are problems with its implementation in practice. There appears to be five themes, or principles, which can guide good strategic planning practice in schools. These are the principles of flexibility, change, involvement, relevance and simplicity.

Flexibility

Strategic planning is not a static process. It must be dynamic and flexible. While it may be a difficult idea to grasp, the plan is out of date as soon as it is written. That means that it can be changed immediately. Plans do not *freeze* into place the directions of change. If conditions change, which prevents the achievement of certain goals, targets should be reviewed. It is unrealistic in today's rapidly changing environment to cast plans in stone. Mechanisms have to be established that enable schools to make rapid reviews and changes.

So, strategic plans need to be living entities. As the school's environment changes, or as a new educational need arises, the school should be able to review its existing strategies and directions and change the plan accordingly.

To illustrate this point, consider what Mrs Lim said to her assistant principal:

■ 'I am at my wit's end. Last December I approved our School Improvement Plan, and we clearly stated that in the first semester this year we would focus our development on implementing the new English curriculum across the school. We said we would allow all teachers to attend the in-service courses, and give them time for preparation of new curriculum materials. Now I am told by the ministry that I have until December this year to implement the First Steps Programme – something or other they have taken from Australia for teaching literacy. How can I do both? I am going to have to tell the staff that the English programme is off – which will of course give them, especially James Chan, the opportunity to say, "We told you that the plan was useless and a waste of time." It is going to make me look like an incompetent'. ■

Mrs Lim finds herself backed into a corner, not because of the ministry's announcement, but because of the ill-conceived strategic planning process she had adopted. Changes – like changes in the priorities of education departments, or in educational policy by governments, or in patterns of need by parents – should be expected. Why should they be so surprising at a time when constant change is the norm? Since strategic planning is about change, it seems rather odd if it is unable to cope with changing circumstances.

Strategic plans, as we said earlier, are about *what should be* and *what could be*, but these must be subject to change. There are two ways in which values based strategic planning builds flexibility into the planning process, and we shall be explaining these in detail later. In general terms, though:

♦ First, flexibility comes from designing the plan around 'focus sheets'. These are developed by staff and parents, with the clearly stated intention that they will change and that they will need to be constantly reviewed. With this in mind, we even recommend the use of loose-leaf binders so that parts of the plan can be easily removed when necessary and replaced.

♦ Second, flexibility comes from the overall cognitive interest developed by the values-based approach to planning. In other words, through the process of involving staff and parents at all stages in the planning process, we seek to engage them in pursuing knowledge about their schools (and their own role in the school) from the perspective of what the school exists to achieve. At all times this is informed by a belief in change. What the school was capable of doing ten years ago or five years ago or what it will be able to do in two years' time are all very different.

Change

Strategic planning is a device about change and for change. If it is done well, it should mean that there is a greater possibility that change will occur successfully, and that schools will be more proactive in seeking to do the things that make them more effective. More important, the continuous development and review of such plans as a regular part of the school's structure should provoke a culture of change and continuous learning. Teachers, in particular, should come to expect change. And change should not be seen as an enemy to be feared but as a force for improved satisfaction and as a part of daily life.

Achieving such lofty ideals is not easy. It is possible, however. Scott (1991), Director General of Education in Queensland, Australia, offers some useful guidance in the form of a planning process which contains three elements:

◆ rational

◆ affective

◆ achievement

Let us look briefly at each of these.

Rational Element

There has to be a recognition of the need for change. This comes from involving staff in gaining new knowledge about the organisation for which they work and from building an understanding of the decisions that constantly need to be made by administration about the dynamics of the school. For example, teachers who spend most of their working week in the classroom should not need to ponder over what the principal does with his or her time. Their involvement in planning should lead them to a greater understanding of how the bits and pieces of the whole work puzzle fit together.

Knowledge is not only about the minutiae of school operations; it may also include an awareness of ministerial mandates, national curriculum issues, new legislation, the rationale for revised administrative procedures, and an understanding of issues relating to enrolment and similar matters. From this perspective, the teacher becomes a genuine stakeholder in the organisation rather than an isolated classroom practitioner. It also means that when teachers gather around certain strategic issues, they are knowledgeable about those issues and have an understanding of their potential impact on the school and its members.

Affective Element

There must also be an acceptance of the need for change. This is best achieved by involving teachers and interested parties from outside the school at all levels in the planning process. Such involvement would include participating in decisions about what in the school they wish to retain, what they want to change and what they want to try out. This is the process of structuring the school in such a way that people can legitimately collect around the key issues which attract their attention. In Section 2, we describe this process in detail.

There is nothing extraordinary about this type of involvement. After all, teachers have a knowledge – seldom expressed openly, admittedly – about what needs to change. With the chance to articulate their views, they can both acknowledge the need for change and become the driving forces for change. This is essential, as we pointed out in discussing strategic issue agendas. The principle here is that wisdom is not the preserve of administrators: it exists throughout the organisation. It must be tapped. Look at these three examples of important knowledge that should lead to change and action:

> ■ All of us who do playground duty have known for ages that something must be done about the bullying and violent behaviour of some of the students – we even know who the students are.
>
> Clearly, from the teachers' perspective, the timetable has to change. Our better students are simply not getting enough time in English or Maths. We can tell you what should be dropped.
>
> It is plain ridiculous. This student got an 'A' in both Biology and Physics, but only a 'C' in Maths; now she has been put in the Arts stream, even though she wants to do Science. Our criteria for streaming students have simply got to change. ■

We are not saying that the teachers are necessarily right, but it is easy to see that they could become the drivers of change if such change is accepted.

Achievement Element

The third element and perhaps the most important in ensuring change is the *belief that change is possible*, and that one can play an important role in bringing it about. In the values-based approach, we tackle this element by enabling staff to see in the final plan how and where they *personally* can play a valuable part in achieving its outcomes.

Involvement

Strategic planning in schools must be based on collaboration, participation and involvement. While there still appears to be a widespread commitment in schools, despite claims to the contrary, to 'boss decides – everyone complies', the problem of imposing vision is that plans become mere rhetoric. Even if people know what they are – and that is seldom the case, it has to be said – they are unlikely to be enthusiastic about seeing them through. People need to feel that their ideas are not only valued but that they also make a real difference.

You will often hear schools declare their allegiance to the ideals of collaboration and wide involvement, but these are usually *espoused* values, and their actions often contradict their words. For example, collaboration usually means one of two things in typical top-down planning:

◆ Wide consultation – This is where the principal announces that the new plan will be based on wide consultation and that everyone will have the opportunity to make an input to the plan. As we all know from our experience, this means that a draft plan will be written and copies will be available in the staff room (or circulated with an 'initial when read' note) to look at. Unless teachers have the energy, willingness or audacity to form a protest group, they usually feel the hopelessness of their situation.

◆ Committees – This is the most common approach to staff participation in schools, and we shall discuss it in detail in a later chapter. Basically, it means the principal declares that a committee or working party is to be formed to develop a strategic plan. This committee may involve various sub-committees that look at aspects of the school. As committees are based on the principle of selected individuals representing the views of others, it enables administrators to claim that the process has been democratic and has ensured widespread involvement.

Neither of these vehicles – consultation or committees – provides the quality of involvement that is needed for meaningful planning. As we said earlier, the real process is less conspicuous and often more informal. People gather around issues which ignite their imagination and which interest them. Quality involvement, therefore, means providing the opportunity for genuine participation as these issues are debated and acted upon.

You will notice that we have concentrated on teachers in talking about involvement. It is indeed a good start to provide quality participation for the professional workforce, but we must not make the mistake of identifying parents and other interested outsiders as merely clients. Their involvement in the planning process is essential if we accept them as members and stakeholders of the broader organisation called a school.

Relevance

Strategic plans must reflect the uniqueness and needs of individual communities and must focus, therefore, not only on systemic requirements. This should not be taken to deny that schools exist as parts of broader systems and are therefore bounded by system requirements and guidelines. For plans to be relevant, they should be predominantly based on and driven by what is valued by the school community.

Simplicity

Traditional top-down approaches to planning in schools appear to have become overly complex and confusing. This is probably because they are based on a scientific approach to planning. The end result can be strategic planning that is characterised by the ubiquitous systems flowcharts, checklists, statistics and algorithms. In many instances, highly complex analysis charts, strategic analysis matrices, needs assessment matrices, cost-benefit analyses, critical path analyses, GANTT Charts, PERT Charts and other such instruments are advanced as being essential to strategic planning. Our belief is that they serve merely to confuse the practitioner and to ensure that the planning consultant, armed with his laptop, remains in work!

It is hardly surprising that people are turned off by the complexity of planning. Plans can be useful without having to bamboozle people. In our values based strategic planning process, we provide a series of steps which will enable the school to develop a strategic plan in just one day. That is somewhat different to those processes which take months to complete. Planning – and this should be music to the administrator's ear – can be short and sweet.

Strategic planning in schools requires flexibility, a culture of change, involvement, relevance and simplicity. All these require skilled and knowledgeable leaders who can ensure there is wide sharing and empowerment amongst those who stake a claim in the well-being of the organisation.

Summary

We have looked at two significant movements in education – the school improvement movement and self-managing schools movement – and at the reasons why schools are necessarily becoming involved in strategic planning. The push towards coherent and effective planning is stronger than ever before.

Strategic planning is the process of deciding *what should be done* and *what could be done*, determining how decisions should be made and what programmes, activities and functions the school can undertake to achieve its values. It is about people taking an interest in and driving certain issues, and it is about doing things which might impact on the school's future condition. A strategic plan must be based on the organisation's uniqueness and on its role. The process must begin with an understanding of what the people who work in or who use the organisational value. Values are defined simply as what people *believe* the organisation exists to achieve.

Strategic plans should be flexible, adaptable to changing circumstances, and relatively simple to develop and implement. Strategic plans are both to achieve organisational values and at the same time to be developed from organisational values. Strategic plans must enable all those involved to see what role they can play in helping the school achieve what it values. Planning must therefore be a shared task amongst all those concerned with the school. It is only when all stakeholders can contribute and think strategically that we can reap the rewards of improved educational opportunities.

CHAPTER 3

Strategic planning and organisational redesign

WE now explore the link between the strategic planning process and the resulting changes that it brings about for the school. Strategic planning, as previously defined, is the process of deciding *what should be* and *what could be* done, of determining how decisions should be made, and of delineating which programmes, activities and functions the school can undertake to achieve what it values. In a nutshell, strategic planning is about change.

In some cases, strategic planning leads to changes which may be relatively minor; in others, it may lead to major organisational redesign. This is something which has to be faced. The school may have to be reshaped in different ways as it discovers that its structure or processes are incompatible with what the school is seeking to achieve.

Organisational redesign may in itself lead to the need for strategic planning. A government may decide, for example, that a school system is too much a drain on resources or that it is not meeting expectations. Strategic planning may be imposed to find ways of reducing costs and increasing effectiveness.

In this chapter, we shall explore the issue of organisational redesign and how it might stem from strategic planning. We look at three models of redesign which have had a considerable impact on schools and other organisations in recent years: restructuring, reengineering and rethinking. Of these three ways of conceptualising organisational change, it is the third process – rethinking – which is embedded in an understanding of values. We shall show, therefore, how it presents the most useful and potentially enduring process of change.

A Fear of Restructuring

Strategic planning, in the minds of many, has been linked to job losses through a process known as 'restructuring'. That is a commonly used term when an organisation undergoes change. Strategic management has generally led to organisational redesign, which in turn has presented an opportunity to consider whether certain jobs are necessary. The economic rationalist paradigm of doing more with less, of cost cutting efficiency drives and of increased accountability, linked with changes in technology, has meant that strategic planning and the subsequent 'restructuring' have been almost entirely associated with changing work practices with the intention of reducing labour costs. It is not surprising that the threat of restructuring strikes terror into the hearts of many people.

A more positive view of strategic planning and resulting organisational redesign comes from Hallinger (1987), who notes an example from the precision metal work industry:

■ Twelve years ago this industry was known quite widely as the Four Ds – workers in the industry worked in Dirty Dark Dangerous Dungeons. The work was highly repetitive and routine, involved hard physical motor skills, required that workers could follow step-by-step directions, and if they could count and read it was a bonus. Now the industry is characterised by: problem solving, teamwork, communication skills, math calculation, use of computers, design work, and innovation. (p. 2) ■

The organisational redesign that follows strategic planning has attracted considerable interest of late and has been a significant focus for both organisational theorists and practitioners. In schools, the use of such a wide term as restructuring, however, is problematic, since it has been applied to mean 'any change in programmes, instructional techniques, or teaching arrangements'

(Greer and Short, 1994, p. 144); as Lieberman and Miller (1990) note, serious students of change in schools have shown a lack of consensus regarding the term's definition. Schlechty (1991, p. 144) too observes that 'widespread confusion and lack of understanding have resulted from the many definitional perspectives'.

To make sense of the concept, we differentiate between various forms of organisational redesign, and to do this we adopt Keidel's (1994) typology, which divides forms of redesign into *restructuring, reengineering* and *rethinking*. We will examine each of these forms. As an overview, Table 3.1 is an attempt by Keidel to sort and classify what he calls the clutter of organisational design processes.

Restructuring in Schools

Restructuring is perhaps the most basic form of organisational change. It occurs when a school undertakes to change its organisational chart. In other words, restructuring involves changing the organisational units (such as departments), positions of responsibility (year heads, assistant principals), or hierarchical structure of the school. This may involve combining, expanding, creating, reducing or eliminating existing units. The following are potted examples of restructuring:

◆ As a consequence of its *School Improvement Plan* entitled *Towards the 21st Century*, Tung Low Secondary School decides to restructure by combining its existing Maths, Science and Technical Studies faculties to form one Technology faculty. In the process, two teachers are told that their services are no longer required.

◆ After its 'review', St Anthony's decides it no longer needs three assistant principals. It elects to change the management hierarchy and to have an administration comprising a principal and two deputy principals. It decides that the work can be handled by adding one more senior teacher to the top team and redistributing the existing assistant principals' tasks between the senior teachers. The three people who were employed as assistant principals now have to reapply for the two remaining deputy principal posts if they wish to retain their status.

Table 3.1 A Classification of Organisational Design Processes

	Restructuring	Reengineering	Rethinking
Metaphors	downsizing rightsizing delayering	process management process innovation process redesign	framing patterning learning organisations
Target	organisational units & hierarchy	business functions & work assignments	individual, group & organisational mindset
Nature	numerical	technical	conceptual
Rationale	survival or repositioning	tactical competitiveness	strategic advantage
Beneficiaries	shareholders	shareholders & customers	shareholders, customers and employees
Performance criteria	efficiency	efficiency & customer satisfaction	efficiency, customer satisfaction & employee development
Organisational variables addressed	control	control & autonomy	control, autonomy and co-operation
Method	computing ratios	flowcharting work processes (interdependencies)	modelling organisation as a balance of multiple perspectives
Upside	reduced costs	simpler, faster work processes	richer planning, decision making & innovation capabilities
Downside	organisational trauma	organisational anxiety	organisational frustration

Source: Keidel (1994, p. 14).

◆ Landlow Primary School has completed its *Action Plan for School Improvement*. A recommendation in the plan is to redistribute the work of school assistants. Instead of being attached to teacher faculties (such as the library or early childhood sections) they are withdrawn to work in a central location with the administrative support unit.

These are simple examples of restructuring. In these cases the changes may be beneficial to the overall operation of the school, but they have resulted from simple arithmetical, scientific managerial thinking and are planned as a means of achieving cuts in spending rather than improvements in learning and teaching. Indeed, economic considerations and staff–student ratios often dominate restructuring.

The school may need to restructure because of falling enrolments or changes in demand patterns, such as students opting for certain courses and not others. Often, however, restructuring can be seen as a knee-jerk reaction to stakeholders' demands for change. For example, a school community may press for radical changes in the way things are managed because of one year's poor examination results. This may lead to restructuring efforts which include moving teachers into different areas of work. Here is a not too untypical memorandum from a principal:

■ | From January, Mr Leung, previously deputy head of the Junior School, will be responsible for our After-school Examination Revision Programme. The Junior School will no longer have a deputy to co-ordinate its activities; the teachers in that section will now come directly under the deputy head for staffing matters. ■

How much of a change is this? Is it merely cosmetic? Or does it improve the students' education?

In both private and public sector organisations, restructuring is the most common form of organisational redesign that comes as a consequence of strategic planning. The labels of retrenchment, downsizing or rightsizing are commonly used to reduce salary bills. It is unfortunate that restructuring has been considered synonymous with economic belt tightening when so much good change has emerged from skilfully implemented restructuring efforts.

Reengineering in Schools

Strategic planning may also result in organisational redesign, which is best described by the term 'reengineering'. This concept was introduced by Hammer and Champy in 1993 and since then has taken the business world by storm. It has had a significant impact on many organisations in Asia. According to Hammer and Stanton (1995, p. 3), reengineering is 'the fundamental re-thinking and *radical redesign* of business *processes* to bring about *dramatic* improvements in performance' (emphasis in original). Whereas restructuring is concerned with moving, shrinking or eliminating organisation units, reengineering is about changing the way work is carried out. As Hammer and Stanton (1995) emphasise, reengineering is neither shedding workforce numbers nor restructuring:

> ■ Reengineering is not downsizing. Downsizing means getting rid of people and jobs to improve short term financial results. Reengineering has nothing in common with that kind of super-ficial and reactive response to problems. Reengineering is about rethinking work from the ground up in order to eliminate work that is not necessary and to find better ways of doing work that is.
>
> Reengineering is also not 'restructuring', usually a euphemism for moving boxes around on an organisational chart or selling off some business units. Reengineering is centred on how work is done, not how the organisation is structured. (p. 10) ■

Reengineering is thus about examining and changing processes or the way work is carried out. This has major implications for strategic planning. An example of reengineering in the schools context is drawn from a region of the Northern Territory of Australia, where the Department of Education undertook a strategic planning review. The resulting document, *Towards the 90s*, found that in order to meet the needs of the community, the total secondary school system would have to be reengineered. The strategic plan changed a system which originally consisted of six comprehensive secondary schools (with students from years 7–12) to a system with one senior college (years 11–12 only), four junior high schools (years 7–10) and one remaining comprehensive school. This meant total reengineering (over six weeks!) for the five schools that changed. It meant new ways of conceptualising timetabling, new curricula, new staff and staffing formulae, right down to making physical changes to buildings. The result of this strategic plan was not a restructuring exercise, but a major reengineering of secondary education.

We can see from examples so far that strategic planning can lead to superficial changes, to restructuring, or to fundamental reengineering of the organisation or the system in which it resides.

There are three terms in reengineering which will help us to understand how the concept relates to strategic planning in schools: sequential interdependence, pooled interdependence, and reciprocal interdependence:

■ *Sequential interdependence*: This is best thought of as an assembly line, with teachers interacting in a chain to give a cumulative effect to their work. Teachers (or groups of teachers) build on the work of the teachers before them. Similarly, students progress from one level to the next (often regardless of their achievement), and this progression is based usually on age.

Pooled interdependence: Where pooled interdependence is low, teachers and staff may be relatively independent of one another. While each teacher provides a discrete contribution to the school, he or she works behind closed doors. The Early Childhood section, for example, may be independent of the Upper Primary. In a secondary school, the Science department may never talk to, never mind work with, the Languages department.

Reciprocal interdependence: This is where teachers and staff interact in a 'back-and-forth' manner, making joint contributions to the learning of the students as a whole. ■

In simple terms, reengineering is about decreasing sequential interdependence and increasing pooled interdependence by minimising the need for 'hands off' between different functions, units or departments. It is also about increasing reciprocal interdependence processes across the school. This shift can be seen in the current emphasis in Australia on the importance of National Student Profiles, Competency Based Assessment and Training (CBAT) and Recognition (or Accreditation) of Prior Learning (RPL or APL). Profiling, for example, can decrease sequential interdependence by allowing children within one class to work at different levels of achievement in various subject areas and at different levels from other students in their class. This can serve to minimise 'hands off' methods, characterised by traditional approaches to learning that may be limited to particular chronological stages of schooling.

Increasing pooled interdependence has recently taken the form of power decentralisation. In previous cases of devolution, central authorities passed budget and financial matters to school leaders. Some principals have taken this a step further and devolved resource decisions within the school, thus making sub-units like departments and sections more interdependent. In some schools, this increased interdependence has taken the form of mini-schools, with their own timetables, staffing and, in the more radical cases, teaching methodologies.

Reciprocal interdependence has taken the forms of increased emphases on team teaching, the use of collaborative approaches to learning, team management, and inclusion policies such as mainstreaming the disadvantaged.

Rethinking in Schools

We have seen how strategic planning may lead to restructuring in some cases and to reengineering in others. At a more radical level, it may lead to completely rethinking the school's purpose.

In the same way that reengineering built on and even subsumed restructuring, rethinking takes planning and change to a higher plane and challenges many of the assumptions which school communities hold about themselves. The basis of this way of thinking strategically is that, before we can redesign schools, we need to redesign the way we think. Such thinking is about the school and its purpose, about the nature of work and about issues such as the role of parents and families. In rethinking, we begin to see the basis of values based strategic planning.

In the values-based approach, the issue underlying the need for organisation redesign is not the restructuring question of 'What structures can we change that would make this school more cost effective or productive?' Nor is it the reengineering question of

'What are the processes that need to change in order for the school to be more effective?' Rather, we need to look to a different cognitive interest, and we might ask something along these lines: 'What is the purpose of the school? What does it exist to achieve? What needs to change in order that this might happen?' These are the questions which are at the heart of rethinking organisations.

The simplest form of strategic plan rethinking can be explained as having three elements. The first is a rethinking of identity: what it stands for. The second element is a rethinking of purpose and interests: this involves asking questions about benefits and purposes, and about whose interests, demands and expectations the school should serve. The third element is concerned with the institution's methods and capabilities: questions about how successfully the school satisfies its clients and fulfils its charter or mission.

The following case study explains how strategic planning may result in rethinking the values of a school:

> ■ Lau Chi Kin School is an established comprehensive school that has been serving the needs of its community and several primary schools for over twenty years but is challenged when demographics change. The young families which once dominated the community no longer live in the area, and consequently the student population has dwindled to the point where the school is threatened with closure. The problems facing the school may be seen as an opportunity for 'rethinking' the school rather then addressing issues about its impending closure. ■

- ◆ First, the school rethinks and changes its notion of a school day, now arranging teaching from early morning to midday.

- ◆ Then, it rethinks the student concept and introduces award-bearing vocational education as well as its mainstream secondary education.

- ◆ The school rethinks the notion of purpose. Its charter is no longer simply to get students through secondary stage examinations but to provide a continuous education service for all ages.

- ◆ It rethinks its capabilities, seeking corporate sponsorship, direct links to industry and ties to tertiary institutions.

This case illustrates well what we were saying in Chapter 2. A major strategic issue was forced onto the agenda, that of impending closure. The school interpreted it as an opportunity: a chance to rethink what role the school might play in a substantially different context to the one in which it had previously operated. And its concern was not so much with what it would do tomorrow as with what actions it could take here and now to influence tomorrow.

This example, of course, may be entirely unrealistic in other contexts, but it serves to illustrate the very different level of thinking that may be called for as schools think and plan strategically. Clearly, the strategic directions explored in that example are of a higher level of complexity than would be called for in restructuring or even reengineering the institution.

Rethinking involves challenging our most basic value assumptions about schools and reinforces the need for us to be concerned with planning at the strategic level. Resultant changes may incorporate both restructuring and reengineering efforts. Since rethinking addresses the fundamental understanding of the school as an organisation and its place in the community, it places values at the centre of the agenda. Thus, people's beliefs, preferences and opinions are brought to bear on important decisions about the school's declared intent for the future. The final part of the book will be devoted to an approach to institutional planning which seeks to understand the complex range of values at play as decisions are taken about what we should do to face a challenging and unpredictable future.

Summary

We have explored the link between the strategic planning process and the resulting changes that it brings about for the school. Strategic planning for school improvement often necessitates organisational redesign, which means reshaping the school in different ways. As schools consider what they are trying to achieve, they may reach the conclusion that their structures and processes are incongruent with their purposes. In some cases, they even conclude that what they are trying to do needs changing. We have explored three concepts which have had a significant impact on organisational redesign, namely, restructuring, reengineering and rethinking. While the first two may have their place, they fail to address the issue of values, and it is for that reason that rethinking provides the most useful vehicle for influencing change that is embedded in the values of the organisation.

CHAPTER 4

Leadership and strategic planning

LEADERSHIP plays a pivotal role in strategic planning. In this chapter we explore the nature and role of leadership in relation to strategic planning in schools. Leadership is a subject which has attracted and continues to attract probably more interest than any other dimension of organisational life. It is also one of the most frustrating, paradoxical and misunderstood concepts in the management literature. It is frustrating because, despite decades of writings on leadership and leader effectiveness, in reality we have got little further than an intuitive understanding of what leaders should be and should do. It is paradoxical because, in a dynamic and unstable context, it is unlikely that leaders can actually lead. We can find no suitable word to explain a role characterised by provoking, learning, challenging, providing ambiguity, creating chaos, promoting difference and intervening. There are other things too, but those few actions give a flavour of effective leading in the new context. And leadership is misunderstood because we have become too entranced by the ubiquitous theoretical framework and we try to put people into appropriate boxes instead of seeking to understand why they do the things they do. Perhaps what is needed is an explanation of leading rather than leadership.

If the leader's role in our present context of education is complex and not clearly defined, we can nevertheless provide useful guidance which will enable leaders to manage strategically and to address the key issues which might find their way onto the agenda.

One metaphor we might use for an effective leader's role is that of 'guide'. In this sense, the leader guides learning by providing an environment alongside stimulus and opportunity, which will enable teachers and members of the community to be involved in an intellectual, practical, ideological and moral analysis of what the school should be doing.

Clearly, such an understanding does not sit well with the traditional view of strong, dynamic leadership. In the army, for instance, it would be anathema to suggest that the strategic battle plan be drawn up through a process of learning from the value preferences of the rank and file rather than by the generals working in isolation. The troops in reality would be told only what they need to know. Even now, many organisations work on the same principle, although changing work practices, changing societal attitudes and the recognition of more enlightened workforces with valuable contributions to make have shifted organisations away from such rigidly authoritarian cultures.

Whatever view of leadership in the contemporary educational context one wishes to adopt, there is at least one feature which is invariably dominant: a leader exerts influence. This influence may be in the form of bringing meaning to the collective actions of others. From this perspective, the importance of hierarchy and position can be de-emphasised and a different emphasis can be placed on the informal networks. These, we argue, are of critical importance to schools in dynamic contexts, and it is the leader's role to support loose networks of informal contacts, since it is these essentially political networks which can handle ambiguity and uncertainty and optimise the output from 'learning communities of practice' (Stacey, 1993).

The Leader's Role in Strategic Planning

Traditionally, the role of the leader in strategic planning has been described in terms of the technical functions he or she must carry out. While functional competence will always be important, strategic leaders must stretch their minds and their actions beyond the day-to-day activities of the organisation.

Leaders need to balance stability and change. They have to think about both the operational and the strategic. They must both consider the operational, day-to-day activities of running their schools and reflect deeply (and act) upon those tasks which define the uniqueness of the school and the role it fulfils in its environment.

Earlier in this book, we described how strategic planning may result in one of three forms of organisational redesign. These may be seen as a continuum ranging from basic structural changes (restructuring) to changes in the processes of the school (reengineering) and deeper changes that challenge the school to rethink its values, character, constituencies and capabilities (rethinking). Part of the leader's role is to do everything possible to position the school in such a way that it might take full advantage of its strategic opportunity. Seen in this light, rethinking, which is embedded in the values and purposes of the school, is the most compelling form of organisational redesign.

The role of the leader, then, in a values-based approach to planning is to involve the school community and to encourage it to view the school in different ways in a constant search for improvement and learning. At the same time, the institution's ongoing existence has to be ensured, so those critical tasks which are part of the day-to-day operations must be given adequate attention. The role of strategic leadership is to explore and define boundaries and tensions as they influence the school's position. Before leaders can do this, however, they themselves must be able to understand how they arrive at decisions about what is important to them. They need to understand how they frame their view of the world.

Strategic Planning and Learning Organisations

Another way of describing the values approach to strategic planning that leads to rethinking organisations is through the concept of 'generative learning', which is promoted in conditions that support a learning culture.

Senge (1990) suggests that the only viable organisations in the 1990s and beyond will be those that have become learning organisations. A learning organisation is one:

> ■ that is continually expanding its capacity to create its future. For such an organisation, it is not enough merely to survive. 'Survival learning' or what is more commonly titled 'adaptive learning' is important – indeed it is necessary. But for a learning organisation 'adaptive learning' must be joined by 'generative learning', learning that enhances our capacity to create. (p. 14) ■

Developing a culture that supports and reinforces the need for learning demands a valuing of organisational members as individuals with the capacity to learn and to contribute in a worthwhile way to organisational success. Deploying human resources in this way can have a 'transformational' effect, as Pedler, Burgoyne and Boydell (1991, p. 32) note: 'A learning company is an organisation that facilitates the learning of all its members and continuously transforms itself'. At a more practical level, a learning culture is one that encourages people to take risks, make suggestions for improvements, be committed to change and innovation and, perhaps most important, believe in what they are doing and know that what they value is shared by management. From this perspective, the organisation of the future is one in which the culture is based on putting values into action.

Senge's work is echoed in the current thinking on 'educative leadership' (Duignan and MacPherson, 1991). The basic tenet of educative leadership is that school leaders should base their work on what is seen to be best educational practice as opposed to practices that may have been imported from incompatible contexts and may be inconsistent with educational goals. Education is based on learning. School operation, therefore, should be framed by learning. Duignan and MacPherson developed a practical theory of educative leadership within a constantly changing environment. To them, educative leadership emphasises the importance of the culture of the organisation and the concern for values and morals in the administration of education: 'A key point made by the ELP research is that educative leaders have a moral responsibility to play a proactive role in helping communities make sense of

changes in ways that help reform social and political relationships' (p. 4).

To many critical theorists, social reality is constituted by
particular individuals and groups, and they can know reality only
in terms of their own values, meanings and motivations. The key
to this perspective is that educational leadership is about dealing
with people and their practice. In this light, people must not be
seen as machine-like resources, but as individuals with values
and attitudes which can lead to profound change and organisational transformation. This leads us to the conclusion that
successful organisations are ones where people truly believe in
what they are doing, since their actions emerge from values.
This is the essence of the school as a learning organisation, and
it is the essence of values based strategic planning.

We want to go back for a moment at this stage to the learning
organisation, for there are several observations we need to make
before driving our discussion forward. One of the main problems
with the learning organisation concept, as attractive as it has
been for many organisations, is its reductionist approach. And
there has been a belief that individual learning will in some
miraculous way lead to transformation at the organisational level.
In a sense, this makes the organisation a separate entity from its
members. As Argyris and Schon (1978) argue, an organisation is
not a 'static separate entity but dynamic and forever changing
– i.e., its natural state is transformation'. You cannot begin to
understand a learning organisation until you begin to examine
your own beliefs about the nature of learning and about the nature
of organisations, and then try to represent those beliefs in some
way. This is organisation taking place through a process of
relationships within the organisation.

This is, we admit, in danger of becoming too intensely theoretical to have practical utility, but it is important to understanding
the basis of a values approach. Underpinning our position on
planning and change in the present-day context is a belief in the
need to rethink organisations. If we can grasp what chaos and
complexity theories are telling us, the notion of control through
formal structure and hierarchy does not hold. New patterns of
influence have to emerge. That does not mean the manager has
to sit back and wait for things to happen. Rather, the manager

can find ways of creating new contexts (Morgan has given us some pointers already) but he or she cannot predict precisely the form it will take.

We now move our discussion forward to consider several other facets of a values approach to strategic planning. Such a perspective views schools in a different way to traditional scientific management approaches. While the traditional view is one of schools as purposefully constructed rational organisations, an alternative perspective is that schools are the result of human action.

A School Is a Human Invention

Traditional views of organisations were dominated by rational explanations of administrative practice (Simon, 1965). Theorists pursuing Simon's ideas generally explored only the factual basis of choice and ignored value and sentiment as possible springs for human action. Because science could not address the ethical dimensions of decision making, values were excluded from the so-called science of administration, and research, therefore, concentrated on facts and control.

Recent thinking has challenged this perspective and attempted to redress the balance in favour of an administrative role for values and beliefs. Theorists (see Bates, 1982; Greenfield, 1975; and Hodgkinson, 1978) have argued that traditional administrative science has failed for the simple reason that the essential questions of administration are not scientific at all; rather, they are philosophical. Organisations are the nexus of freedom and compulsion. As invented social realities, organisations are both created and manipulated, and both of these, therefore, are part of administration's remit.

The central realities of administration are moral issues – issues that have been camouflaged behind a facade of facts and procedures, such that any sense of responsibility has often been removed. The acknowledgement and clarification of values allow us to recognise that decisions represent something beyond the decisions themselves: they bespeak a value and perhaps even a commitment (Leithwood and Musella, 1991, p. 7).

Greenfield (1975) criticised systems theory for viewing organisations, such as schools, as 'natural' or 'real' systems, suggesting that organisations are only a human 'invented social reality'. He also attacked the theory on the basis it was not feasible to split values from facts. The result of doing so, he claimed, created theory that is of little use to administrators in their work. Greenfield adopted an interpretive or phenomenological view of organisations, claiming that organisations are not goal-oriented natural systems, but rather social creations. In Greenfield's terms, to understand organisations requires that we understand how intention becomes action and how one person's intention and action trigger intention and action in others.

The traditional 'science' of organisations sought to locate and understand the mechanism of control in organisations, hoping that such understanding would enable people to control the mechanism of control (the development of 'laws'). Such mechanisms, though, may sometimes be seen as devices in which an independent 'organisational will' can be forced upon human intention. But, as we have seen, it is individuals who intend, not organisations. This brings us to an important perspective – that people make genuinely free choices and perform free actions, and human behaviour cannot be explained by causal laws and condition but must be valued for what it is: the effect of human values in action. We will come back to this point in a later chapter on values.

As an example of values being translated into action, consider this statement from the chief executive officer of the airline Qantas:

■ We have plans for more initiatives, more improvements, more investment in making our people committed to taking ownership and responsibility for doing things well, every day, in every area of our operation. It takes time, but we will ensure that we strive even harder to involve more and more of our people in every aspect, and do it via interesting and enjoyable events and occasions. It is a great opportunity to benefit doubly, by improving the customer product and services and simultaneously building internal confidence, momentum and sense of going forward. (Strong, 1994, p. 4) ■

The stated values of Qantas as published in their strategic plan are:

■ Qantas believes it should strive to attain an organisational culture built on their employees having:
- ◆ a sense of involvement with participation;
- ◆ a feeling of things happening and momentum;
- ◆ an atmosphere of doing things together;
- ◆ a spreading acceptance of personal responsibility for results; and
- ◆ growing ownership of what happens or does not happen for customers.

(Strong, 1994, p. 4) ■

While these may be only espoused values, and not values in action, it seems clear that the CEO of Qantas believes in the importance of the people in his organisation.

Strategic Planning and the Importance of People

Throughout the 1960s, 1970s and 1980s, it was suggested that a successful organisation was one which had both a visionary leader and a clear strategic plan. The two went hand in hand, the leader providing both the vision of where the organisation hoped to be and the strategic direction, with accompanying detail about how to get there. On the surface, this is unproblematic. Much of the rhetoric about market-leading organisations dwells on paternalistic and charismatic leadership: the culture of 'a man with a mission' (the gender choice is intentional!). On closer inspection, however, it represents a paradigm that is untenable in the 1990s. Why? Because it ignores the importance of people and implies that there is one correct solution, which only the formal leader can identify. Such a view shows scant regard for the knowledge, values, and vision, not to mention wisdom, of the many others who work within the organisation and who know best how the organisation can achieve its key results.

Operating with this philosophy meant that strategic planning was usually based on what may best be described as a 'rolling down' model. The visionary leader (or leaders) produce a picture of the organisation's future, which is usually distilled as a list of key objectives, broad goals, and the ubiquitous mission statement. This vision is passed down the hierarchy to the middle level managers, who are required to establish a plan to conjure the vision into reality. The strategic plan usually takes the form of strategies and action plans, but may also include statements about key values. In order to make this happen, a senior officer would take responsibility for producing this guiding document, or an external consultant would be brought in. The officer or consultant would interview, inspect, observe and converse in preparation for the writing of the plan. This would be known as the 'consultation phase' and would indicate to rank and file that they had an important part to play in determining the organisation's future.

There have been various refinements to this consultation process, where meetings may be held at expensive hotels to ascertain how the workers can successfully fulfil senior management's mission. These meetings are designed to develop commitment and may take the form of bribes (like time off work or a good lunch) or fervent presentations by charismatic individuals schooled in the psychology of the 'warm and fuzzy'. A quaint artefact of this type of strategic process is the insistence that all staff (at all levels) must be able to recite verbatim the firm's mission statement.

In truth, whatever success the 'rolling down' model has enjoyed has had little to do with the scheme but much to do with the positional power and ruthlessness of the leadership. The resulting glossy documents with fancy graphics have usually been discarded or ignored by organisational members.

The impact on the organisation of such imposed models has come not from the plans or their formulation but from the often vicious restructuring, associated with technology and system changes, that accompanied the strategic planning exercise. Consultants (who enjoyed a huge rise in numbers through the 1970s and 1980s) were often quick to establish a relationship between improved economic performance and the commitment of employees to the master strategy. Yet, the profit and efficiency benefits often resulted from shedding staff and improving operational procedures, accompanied by updating technology. Even in the world of commerce, such an approach has little to commend it; much less so in the sphere of education, where only marginal gains can be achieved through such measures.

The notion of hiring visionary leaders who can move in and turn organisations around is being seriously questioned. They may give the impression that radical things are being done, but whether they are able to provide absolute wisdom and account for organisational values, beliefs and performance, and for client demands is debatable. Of course, there may be circumstances in which someone new at the helm can have a dramatic effect on the organisation, but whether such effects are lasting and sufficiently fundamental to impact on the roots of problems must be open to speculation. It makes more intuitive sense that those who actually work in a school are able to devise and implement strategies which might improve student learning, and that leaders can facilitate the process.

It seems that older models of strategic planning, prevalent in the hierarchical structures of previous decades, are out of keeping with contemporary beliefs about teamworking, empowerment and continuous improvement, since they present barriers to effective change (Carr and Littman, 1990; Fullan, 1993; Semler, 1993). They fail to tap the ideas and energies of human resources, and they fail to generate the sort of support needed for successful implementation. The current rhetoric, in contrast, is about locating decisions with those who actually do the job (Carr and Littman, 1990), and this is a persuasive view that has won widespread support.

Schools and their sub-units are the result of human invention. It seems logical that those who operate in them and share their purpose should also share in determining their direction. By valuing people's input, we begin to see how strategic planning may be a way of understanding organisational values and how such values can be transposed into action.

Reframing: A Way of Elevating Understanding

Another understanding of the role of leadership in strategic planning comes from the work of Bolman and Deal (1991) in their theory of leadership frames. They use the notion of frames to capture the idea that as people enter and exit from hundreds of different situations, they define their circumstances in such a way that they know what to do and how to understand what others are doing. They further explain that the frame people choose determines the reality that they experience and provides a script for their actions. This notion of frames aligns with our thinking on values based strategic planning. A strategic plan must be developed within the frame that shapes relevant people's understanding. Plans that are handed down from consultants or from senior management run the risk of adopting inappropriate frames. In other words, the plans become meaningless and irrelevant to those who are charged with implementing them.

Bolman and Deal claim these frames are really intellectual constructs. When school leaders view their organisations (or problems and situations related to the organisation) they typically prefer one frame over another. Strategic leaders learn to deepen their understanding of problems and issues by viewing them through different lenses and thus seeing them in the different ways in which others might view them.

The four frames the authors identify are the *structural*, the *human resource*, the *political* and the *symbolic*. The technical frame is the one most used by leaders. This is not unexpected, since there is a prevalent view that organisations and the events within them are rational, that people's actions and decisions are based on logical reasoning. Looking at situations from such a narrow perspective can constrain thinking about the nature of problems and may well make preferred solutions inappropriate. By viewing situations from several frames of reference, a comprehensive perspective can be obtained, one which gives rise to at least several courses of response or action. The frames, adapted from Bolman and Deal (1991), are outlined below. We have also provided examples of what a leader preferring a given frame may value.

Strategic leaders in the technical frame get their key results through:

- emphasising productivity;
- maximising measurable outcomes;
- establishing clear rules;

- ◆ setting measurable targets and performance indicators; and
- ◆ developing tight control and co-ordination mechanisms.

The results of such an emphasis may include:

- ◆ a high percentage of students passing external examinations;
- ◆ increased financial support through sponsorship;
- ◆ more advanced skills teachers than at other schools; and
- ◆ competitive performance in school sports.

Strategic leaders in the political frame get their key results through:

- ◆ influencing behaviours;
- ◆ nurturing competition for scarce resources;
- ◆ bargaining and reaching compromise amongst interest groups;
- ◆ developing positive conflict between stakeholders;
- ◆ recognising external influences; and
- ◆ developing negotiation throughout the school.

The following may be present:

- ◆ strong networking amongst staff;
- ◆ clear coalitions that are flexible and dynamic;
- ◆ dynamic and constructive conflict; and
- ◆ identifiable and powerful change agents.

Strategic leaders in the human frame get their key results through:

- ◆ highlighting the importance of needs and motives;
- ◆ meeting individual needs;
- ◆ constructing a caring and trusting environment;
- ◆ supporting staff; and
- ◆ encouraging staff involvement in decision making.

The results of such an orientation might include:

- ◆ high staff morale;
- ◆ high staff involvement in the school's activities;
- ◆ high parental and student involvement in school activities;

◆ provision of school activities that meet special needs; and

◆ involvement in courses that meet individual needs (e.g., gifted children).

Strategic leaders in the cultural frame get their key results through:

◆ focusing on the identity of the organisation;

◆ anchoring actions through values;

◆ encouraging shared norms and beliefs;

◆ communicating through symbols, myths, metaphors and stories;

◆ linking the organisation's values with the values of its community; and

◆ building the school around its community's values.

In such a frame, the following are examples of resulting conditions:

◆ school community values are clearly defined and lived;

◆ ceremonies, symbols and myths reinforce school community values;

◆ the school hall is used by the community as a drop-in centre; and

◆ community members teach general hobby courses in the school.

The essence of this conceptual perspective is developing understanding. Leaders who can transpose their thinking to understand what others value and believe in strengthen their own position. It is empowering for both leaders and led if there can be an elevated mutual understanding of the different ways in which people might define organisational purpose. One word connected with purpose that has featured prominently in the contemporary management literature is 'vision'. We now turn our attention to this concept, which, in relation to leadership, has attracted widespread attention.

A New Understanding of Vision

The hallmark of a learning organisation is not lovely visions floating in space, but a relentless willingness to examine 'what is' in the light of our vision (Senge, 1990).

Few would disagree with Saul (1987, pp. 273–280) when he notes that it is no longer good enough to simply administer organisations: managers must lead. The shift from management as administration to management as leadership implies a need to think strategically. It also implies leadership both within and outside the organisation, such that influence is exerted amongst both employees and external stakeholders. The fact that we use the word 'influence' is significant in itself, since it is in stark contrast to the legacy of 'command' inherited from the church and the armed forces. Such a role has been largely discarded in contemporary organisations in favour of one that supports relationships and involvement.

In the new understanding of vision, the leader's role is to enable the vision of the staff to emerge. As Pascale (1990, p. 265) warns: 'Charismatic, high-flying leaders and premature strategic planning are blinding because they distract us from our own possibilities'. The new visionary leader is one who is able to nurture the development of vision from the organisation, from its staff and from what they value. From this angle, vision is seen as a common belief in the organisation's future to which stakeholders can commit themselves. It would be unrealistic to talk about a 'common vision' as such, for it would be illusory. What we can aim for, however, is a willingness to be attracted by a particular vision. In this regard, the leader focuses and synthesises – in a 'rolling up' process – what is believed in and valued by the organisation.

There are other problems too with the notion of a single common vision. Apart from the fact that different things occupy different people's minds, the chances are that these things change over time. They are seldom as permanent as a vision – some perfect state in the future – would imply. Perhaps we should not be looking, therefore, for something that is too strongly shared. Innovations are more likely to emerge from differences and conflict. Stacey (1991, p. 13) notes: 'Innovative strategic moves change the way we do things and this threat to existing frameworks is bound to lead to conflict. Innovation and different values are clearly closely connected. Despite the techniques available for promoting consensus, we observe continuing differences of view, and conflict in companies which are actively doing new things, because without difference and conflict new things are impossible'.

The current understanding of vision, as it has been conventionally explained in the literature, needs to be questioned. Visions may be thought desirable to inform coherent change, but the dominant process of formulation must be challenged. As Fullan (1993, p. 28) states: 'Visions are necessary for success but few are as misunderstood and misapplied in the change process'. He continues:

■ | The question is not whether visions are important; they invariably are, rather, it is how they are shaped and reshaped. They die prematurely if they are mere paper products churned out by leadership teams, when they are static or even wrong, and when they attempt to impose a false consensus suppressing rather than enabling personal visions to flourish. (p. 29) ■

This brings a whole new view to light. Fullan suggests the organisational vision should emerge from rather than precede action, and that it results from the dynamic interaction of organisational members and leaders. In short, he suggests that visions come later in the change process, rather than at the beginning of it, and that 'visioning' should be an open-ended process. But Fullan takes us beyond the notion of a single guiding light and into the realm of multiple visions, which might enable individuals to flourish and which might lead to organisational vitality. Of course, there needs to be an agreement about core purpose, but strength comes from diversity of beliefs, values and personal missions.

We have demonstrated in our work in many schools that organisational vision is best achieved when distilled from the dominant values of the people who form the organisation. Taking this line, a strategic planning process should start, not with a leader's vision, but with the values and beliefs of the school and its community.

Hargreaves (1994, p. 248) too questions the leader's generally accepted role. He cites Achilles' advice as an example of all that is wrong with the concept:

■ | They (leaders) must know how to administer schools to achieve the desired results. As a starting point, principals must envision better schools, articulate this vision to others, and orchestrate consensus on the vision. (Achilles, 1987, p. 18) ■

Much of the current literature reflects this sort of approach, that the leader is responsible for determining institutional direction and for communicating it successfully to the compliant followers; that the school should be organised in line with the mission and that those who are unable to comply should be isolated. In this model, managers prepare forecasts, formulate visions and missions (sometimes at weekend retreats) and then mount comprehensive culture change programmes of persuasion and propaganda in an effort to gain commitment amongst organisational members. Fullan warns, however, that if the beliefs upon which such persuasion is based are unfounded, improvement efforts will be futile. Clarifying values before forming vision, therefore, makes sense. Personal vision is not suppressed; rather, it is valued as an important contribution to innovation and entrepreneurial activity.

The most powerful shared visions are those that contain the basis for further generative learning and recognise that individual and organisational development will always be in dynamic tension. Recognising and valuing this tension are essential (Fullan, 1993, p. 34).

Hargreaves (1994) alerts us to the problem of vision without 'voice':

■ Exclusive emphasis on vision or voice alone is constructive neither for restructuring in general nor for professional development in particular. A world without voice, without vision, is a world reduced to chaotic babble where there are no means of arbitrating between voices, reconciling them or drawing them together ... We have seen that a world of vision without voice is equally problematic. In this world, where purposes are imposed and consensus contrived, there is no place for the practical judgement and wisdom of teachers; no place for their voices to get a proper hearing. A major challenge for educational restructuring is to work through and reconcile this tension between vision and voice; to create a choir from a cacophony. (p. 251) ■

A values-based approach to strategic planning attempts to provide new opportunities for the 'voice' of teachers in the construction of and alignment to vision. Similarly, the understanding of effective strategic planning must take on a new meaning, one based on the voice of people, a voice that has beliefs about how the organisation should approach its future. Ingram (1992) summarises these ideas, and we give him the last word:

> ■ Change that bubbles up from the grassroots has staying power. For best results, the people in the institution must have ownership of the new vision with decisions being made from the bottom-up in a participatory fashion rather than top-down. Rethinking is a constant, long-term process with the word process being emphasised. It is not a product you get or bring in from the outside. It is something that occurs inside an institution (but well instructed by what is going on outside). And it must be a shared vision, a strategic vision. (p. 18) ■

Summary

This chapter has explored the link between leadership and strategic planning. The leader's role is a highly complex one. We have seen how leaders must provoke the anxiety that leads to creative tensions as strategic issues are addressed. From this perspective, the leader encourages and supports people as they take interest in particular issues and deal with them. The leader may also be instrumental in interpreting the environment so that the key issues reach the agenda and are attended to. Thus, strategic leadership is partly about exploring and defining boundaries and tensions as they influence the school's position. Sometimes, the leader has to intervene in organisational processes in order to disturb established patterns. These are all important roles in the new context. Leaders must consider the day-to-day activities of running their schools, as well as reflect deeply on and act upon those tasks which define the uniqueness of the organisation and the role it fulfils in its environment. The role of the leader, then, in values based strategic planning is to involve and encourage the school community to view the school in different ways in a constant search for improvement and learning while, at the same time, ensuring its ongoing existence. This requires a skilful balancing act, one which both provokes anxiety and protects the organisation from too much anxiety, which would lead to debilitating chaos. Leaders are indeed special people with a special role to play, one that is at complete odds with the prevalent hierarchical models with which we are all too familiar.

CHAPTER 5

Strategic thinking

A strategic plan is of no consequence if the people who must make it happen cannot think strategically. In this chapter, we explore strategic thinking and ways in which school leaders can involve staff in strategic exercises at the classroom level. We shall establish ways in which the personnel who have key parts to play in schools – teachers, administrators, parents and many others – can become shareholders in the school's strategic direction and intent.

A common response by teachers when given a copy of the school's grand plan – whatever it may be called – is one of complete indifference, since they see it as having no relevance to their lives as classroom teachers. Plans, to them, are for the principal and other members of the management elite to dream up, since they (members of the executive) are paid to deal with those sorts of things. However, the purpose of a school's strategic plan is to improve educational outcomes, and this cannot happen if the very people who have to make the changes do not see that they have a role in its implementation. Perhaps the main reason for such indifference is that teachers are not encouraged to think strategically. They are protected by their classroom isolation from the 'big picture' of school plans. Some like it this way; others have no choice.

We shall provide concrete ways in which school leaders can help teachers and others – including parents and students – to think strategically. In support of a values-based approach to planning, we provide you with a system of strategic thinking centred around several strategic exercises: the seven planning hexagons; critical operating tasks versus strategic management tasks; and the principle of critical success factors.

But let us start with a story:

■ Mrs Lim could not understand what all the fuss was about. Her school was to become what the department called a self-managing school, and part of this, she was told, was that she had to work on a school development plan. This puzzled her, as, in her opinion, she had always done planning. Now the department was sending out all sorts of memos telling her *how* she should plan and *why* she should plan. What was even more frustrating was that no one was telling her what the basis of her plans should be. As far as she was concerned, she already did planning properly – she had programme plans, staff deployment plans, curriculum plans, plans for school excursions and plans for improving student behaviour. What was all the fuss about? She knew what she was doing in her school and she always had done. The school was operating very smoothly, thank you very much! ■

Mrs Lim had not previously been called on to map out a preferred future for her school. Planning for her had only ever needed to address the technical or day-to-day issues of the school. She was not aware that, in being asked to write a school development plan, she was being asked to do something different. Mrs Lim was not accustomed to thinking strategically. She did not see plans as anything but mechanisms for dealing with today's issues and problems.

Mrs Lim is probably not alone in her frustration. For principals who have been used to working in a stable, centrally controlled school environment, planning has basically involved making sure that things are running smoothly and are 'under control'. In other words, in traditional, centralised systems, planning has been the device for ensuring that what needs to happen on a day-to-day basis actually happens. Planning for the school's open day, planning for the end of year examinations, and planning for next year's staffing needs – all of these are commonplace processes for ensuring that nothing goes wrong, that everything is predicted and all factors controlled (as far as is humanly possible). While such plans are very important and form a significant part of the work of managers, they are not strategic plans.

In the following pages, we begin to alleviate Mrs Lim's confusion by addressing the various levels of planning in her school and by emphasising the importance of engaging all staff in strategic thinking. As we described in Chapter 1 in the story of Wayne Gretzky – 'I skate to where I think the puck will be' – strategic plans are of little value if the staff who have to implement them are not equipped to think strategically. Teachers must be able to step out of their classrooms to think strategically, and parents must be able to articulate a wider concern than that which is just for their child's classes and education.

Strategic Thinking

In simple terms, strategy is about positioning yourself to take advantage of your situation. The word 'strategic' is best understood as relating to the uniqueness of the organisation and the role it might best fulfil in its environment.

Strategic thinking on the part of teachers and the broader school community means that they are able to engage with the strategic intent of the school in ways that empower them to question what should be going on, what could happen and what is needed to achieve those things that are highly valued by the school. There needs to be a balance between stability and change. Stability is evident in the day-to-day activities of work existence, but it may conceal the more complex and uncertain role which the organisation has to enact in its environment. Involvement with both is important.

Every school plans. Yet, rarely do teachers or parents have more than a peripheral involvement in the development of plans. Sometimes, they are not even aware they exist. To illustrate this point, ask yourself the following questions:

♦ In my school, what would happen if a child was to have a major accident in the playground? What plan of action would we follow?

♦ What are my school's future capital works plans? What buildings are next to be repainted, or what changes need to be made to classrooms?

- ◆ What plans are in place to deal with students' special educational needs?

- ◆ What plans are in place for incorporating computers and technology into our teaching?

Assuming you have the plans, who made them? Where are they located? Who is responsible for their review and implementation? In many cases, and especially if we were asking teachers those questions, the answer would be, 'I'm not quite sure. I guess the principal has them and knows what's happening'.

You may well argue that teachers do not need to know about these things. Surely, the painting schedule – or upgrading the classroom environment, if you prefer – is important only to the principal or school bursar? That may be true, but the key issue here is promoting strategic thinking. The process of being involved and empowered is a vital one.

The extent of strategic thinking is usually restricted to the submission of lesson plans or teaching programmes for the next term or semester. In such situations, it is hardly surprising if the release of the new strategic plan is greeted by total disinterest or disdain. It may also help to explain why teachers are seen as being resistant to change: their experience of it is as the victims of edicts from on high.

The Seven Planning Hexagons

One strategy for getting staff involved in thinking strategically is to promote the use of 'planning hexagons'. Based on the work of Bryson (1989) we have developed what we call the 'seven planning hexagons'. These are simple cognitive devices, or thinking tools, that help people to plan activities or programmes.

As an example of how they work, consider the following case:

■ At St Andrew's, the senior teacher, Paul Chang, who co-ordinates the Early Childhood teachers, decided to use planning hexagons in the regular professional development session. The teachers meet every second Thursday for 90 minutes for different professional development activities. This time, Paul asked the teachers to develop a planning hexagon around the issue of improving their classroom practice. He gave out the format of the planning hexagon, and the five teachers brainstormed how to complete the diagram. By the end of the session, they produced six different planning hexagons on how to improve their classroom practice. Three of the teachers continued to develop a further three planning hexagons over the following four weeks and then presented their work to the group. ■

Some examples of their findings included planning hexagons for:

◆ co-ordinating classes in such a way as to enable the teachers to segregate boys and girls during Science and Maths lessons every morning for a period of ten weeks;

◆ adopting a change in the way poor behaviour was dealt with, including the setting up of a time-out desk, where badly behaved students would sit and all teachers would be able to see what they were doing; and

◆ investigating new approaches to maths teaching that encompassed competency-based teaching methods.

These plans were illustrated on A3-sized posters that were put up around the staff room.

In the example of the hexagon shown in Figure 5.1, the teachers either individually or as a group were asked to develop a plan that would lead to improved classroom practice in the Early Childhood area of the school. The planning hexagon directed them to consider why, what, when, where, who and how they could improve what they were doing in the context of both the structure and the culture of the classroom. They were to write on the hexagon itself at the appropriate points. In this professional development session, the teachers were being asked to think strategically. They thought about what they valued (what they saw as improved classroom practice) and how it could be attained.

Planning hexagons are based on a belief that plans are derived from the culture and structure of the organisation.

■ *Culture* refers to the values that anchor the decisions made within the organisation. It refers to the beliefs and understandings that people share about the practices and behaviours that are acceptable.

Figure 5.1 Planning Hexagon

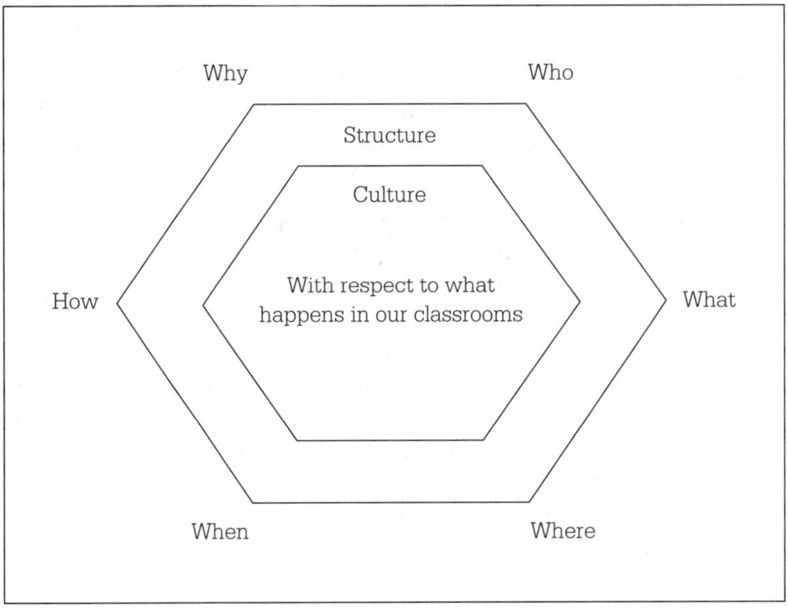

Why   Who

Structure

Culture

How   With respect to what   What
             happens in our classrooms

When   Where

> *Structure* refers not just to the physical conditions and re-
> sources, but also to the rules and resources people use when
> interacting. Some examples of structures might be the stores
> of knowledge that an individual has about interaction in
> general (grammar rules, social norms), combined with his or
> her knowledge of a specific organisation (organisation chart,
> standard procedures, common acronyms). These are the rules
> and resources – *structures* – that individuals can draw upon to
> achieve their own goals. (Giddens, 1984) ■

A useful way of providing a framework for strategic thinking is
placing operational plans in seven categories. They relate to:

◆ what happens in our classrooms;

◆ human resource management and development;

◆ our management practices;

◆ our community relations and client service;

◆ our buildings and other capital resources;

◆ financial resources; and

◆ risk management.

These categories are not prioritised, since each is as important as the other. Schools need to have staff involved in strategic thinking that encompasses all seven areas of concern. Not all staff need to develop planning hexagons in all areas, but they should be involved in those planning hexagons which impact on their roles and responsibilities. Teachers should not be excluded from planning that has traditionally been the domain of the school bursar or registrar, but should have the opportunity to be involved in a wide range of strategic concerns.

Another example of how the planning hexagons can be used is given in the following case:

■ At St Andrew's, the assistant principal asked every senior teacher (department head or coordinator) to involve *all* of their staff in developing a planning hexagon about occupational health and safety, and risk management. This was to be done at their regular staff meeting. They were given the hexagon shown in Figure 5.2 with an accompanying list of questions designed to prompt their thinking. ■

Figure 5.2 Planning Hexagon for Occupational Health and Safety, and Risk Management

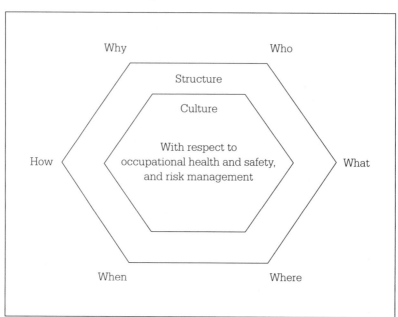

The questions were, what happens if:

◆ there is a fire in the school?

◆ a student falls off a climbing frame and is badly hurt?

◆ the high-interest financial investments of the school collapse?

◆ the school bus rolls over while on an excursion?

◆ a parent takes his child away at lunch time, but he does not have legal custody?

◆ one of our religious instruction volunteers turns out after ten weeks to have been completely crazy?

◆ a parent takes legal action against us for libel?

In this example, the assistant principal is using the occupational health and safety, and risk management planning hexagon to force teachers to think about these highly pertinent issues. They are thinking strategically.

While every school may have a critical incidents plan for dealing with such things as school ground accidents, as every school practitioner will know, it is all too often the case that the staff will not even be aware of its existence, let alone what is in it. Having staff involved in such strategic exercises paves the way for the school to undertake major strategic planning processes.

Strategic Management Tasks versus Critical Operating Tasks

Another strategy for getting staff involved in thinking strategically is to distinguish between strategic management tasks and critical operating tasks. We have adapted this way of strategic thinking from Kiggundu (1989), who suggests that organisations need to distinguish clearly between their strategic and operating tasks and to ensure that both are being given adequate attention.

Critical Operating Tasks

Critical operating tasks are those basic tasks which must be performed by an organisation to ensure its existence and through which it strives to achieve its mission. Such tasks would probably be familiar to Mrs Lim. Typical critical operating tasks include:

- organising an effective timetable;
- establishing acceptable classroom practices;
- ensuring the curriculum is set;
- monitoring teachers' programmes;
- establishing effective assessment and reporting procedures;
- establishing an effective records and school information system;
- scheduling teacher professional development; and
- setting a playground duty roster.

Strategic Management Tasks

Strategic management tasks are those tasks that define the uniqueness of the organisation and the role it fulfils within its environment. Depending on the school's culture, these might include such tasks as:

- developing a mission statement;
- defining the values and beliefs of the teachers and other staff of the school;
- defining the organisation's critical success factors (what constitutes success for the school);
- writing action plans for school improvement;
- establishing a School Council with real powers to influence the school's direction;
- assessing the impact of the school on its community;
- surveying the student body to understand its needs and values;
- decentralising decision making within the school to ensure input of all staff;
- encouraging staff to review position descriptions;
- rethinking school timetables; and
- empowering staff to talk to parents and community about their needs.

Strategic management tasks and critical operating tasks should be undertaken simultaneously. It is important that neither is undervalued. The usual picture is one of strategic management tasks being given only cursory attention. This is understandable, since the day-to-day operational tasks are immediate concerns and, in comparison to strategic issues, require less cerebral activity. However, if the strategic concerns are not given sufficient attention, schools tend to be chaotic and largely ineffective. They are the schools that spend their time dealing with one crisis after another, getting students into classes, hurriedly getting teachers' programmes sorted out, dealing with discipline catastrophes and trying to stop leaking plumbing. Senior administrators spend time running around the school 'putting out fires' and attempting to solve other people's problems for them. Perhaps such people should heed a new proverb we have introduced into the planning dictionary: 'a minute spent on strategic management tasks will save a day on critical operating tasks'!

An interesting side effect of the push towards 'heroic' leadership in the 1990s was the emergence of schools whose leadership moved to concentrate almost solely on strategic management tasks at the expense of critical operating tasks. These were schools where leadership became highly entrepreneurial and highly future-focused and visionary, often at the expense of the critical day-to-day operations. Staff would complain that the principal was seldom in school but spending time at regional or national meetings, or at Rotary events or departmental committees. They may even have complained that resources were spent on activities designed to raise the school's profile, such as parades and sponsorship events. A common outcome of such an approach to leadership was that the principal realigned the purpose of the school without asking or even telling anyone. Meanwhile the student absenteeism report system was totally unreliable, a science teacher was teaching senior maths to a class of three students, and the A Block toilet was out of commission pending an inspection by the Health Department.

The underlying principle of strategic management tasks versus critical operating tasks is that effective schools pay equal attention to both operating and strategic tasks. This principle underpins the encouragement of strategic thinking amongst teachers.

Using Critical Operating Tasks versus Strategic Management Tasks to Promote Strategic Thinking

An example of how critical operating tasks versus strategic management tasks can be used to promote strategic thinking in a school can be seen in the following case:

■ | The principal of St Andrew's, Mrs Lim, asked each of the senior teachers to develop a business plan for one aspect of teachers' concern in their area. Mrs Lim gave each of the senior teachers a proforma that described what the business plan should contain and the instruction that 'the business plan should set out the issues of importance that are identified by your staff as impacting on their area of work; they can focus on critical operating tasks or on strategic initiatives'. ■

Initially, the response was poor, as teachers discovered that they had no experience or expertise in writing business plans. In fact, they had never been asked to think strategically before. The principal then arranged a series of in-service workshops for staff during their professional development meetings. Figure 5.3 shows an example of a business plan developed by teachers.

Asking staff to be involved in the development of such business plans serves two purposes: first, it involves staff in strategic thinking. In the absentee report system example, it resulted in teachers expressing their concern for the issue, because they valued caring for students and felt that this value was not currently being achieved.

Second, the exercise involved teachers in thinking about critical operating tasks. In this case, the critical operating tasks centred on the legal and administrative processes of reporting student absenteeism.

Overall, the strategic exercise was successful. Not only did Mrs Lim engage her staff in strategic thinking, but she was also able to develop the skill of writing business plans, a more than useful competency in an era of economic rationalism and self-managing schools.

Figure 5.3   Business Plan to Establish a Student Absenteeism Reporting Programme

Objective

To augment the existing school information system with a computer-based programme that will enable student absenteeism to be notified to parents within 24 hours.

Rationale

Currently, the process of data gathering on student absenteeism and data entry both result in absentee reports being available to teachers, counsellors and administrators within five days.

The school has received many complaints from parents because of the delay in notification.

Key Tasks

Computer faculty senior staff to establish Student Absenteeism Database on desktop computer using the software program '4D'. Completion date: 30 June.

Registrar to establish a staff rotation schedule for school assistants to enter data at the end of school each day. Completion date: 30 June.

Computer faculty senior staff to conduct training programmes for staff on Student Absenteeism Database on desktop computer using the software program '4D'. Completion date: 30 July.

Assistant principal (staffing) to administer collection of green absentee forms ('greenies') from all teachers at the end of each lesson. Start date: 1 August.

Absentee reports to be generated nightly, with student attendance reports being placed in teachers' pigeon-holes by assistant principal (staffing) every morning before Homeroom. Start date: 1 August.

Cost

Computer hardware and software	$35,000
Ongoing maintenance costs	$1,500 annual
Overtime costs	$10,000 annual

Budget Implications

Initial cost of $46,500 for next year can be met from New Initiatives Grant, as the project aim to reduce absenteeism is within departmental guidelines. Recurring costs can be met within existing budget.

Personnel

Implications for workload of assistant principal (staffing) and school assistants on rotation.

School Assistants Award enables payment of overtime for work conducted outside school hours.

Performance Indicators

By the extent that

◆ the computer system is operational by 1 August 1998

◆ the reporting of student absenteeism is within 24 hours by 30 August 1998

Review and Evaluation

Computer faculty senior staff and assistant principal (staffing) to deliver a report on the operation of the system at the general staff meeting on 30 August 1998.

Strategic Management Tasks and Organisational Structures

Another example of how critical operating tasks versus strategic management tasks can be used to develop strategic thinking amongst staff comes from the use of the word 'strategic' in strategic management tasks. While it may suggest a concern with future-oriented activities, this is not the only focus. Strategic management tasks are also about understanding environment issues, values, cultures and the organisation's structures.

An important type of strategic management task is that which is concerned with a continuous analysis of the organisation's structure as a means of understanding the uniqueness of the organisation and, strategically, how best to utilise this understanding to build a more effective organisation. By 'structures' we do not mean the physical facilities, but rather the rules and resources which people in the organisation use in their day-to-day interaction (Giddens, 1984). Structures provide the framework within which individuals can interact meaningfully. They are created by the organisation's people.

Possibly the best way to think about structures is to consider the stores of knowledge that an individual has about interaction in general (what people know about grammar rules, social norms, what you can and cannot say in the staff room, and so on) and combine these with the individual's knowledge of a specific organisation (organisational chart, standard procedures, common acronyms used in the school, who is important). This is the basis for the rules and resources – *structures* – upon which people draw to achieve their goals. Structures recursively organise everyday life and practices in schools. From this standpoint, learning to understand structures is an important strategic management task.

As an example of how this might be put into practice, the school's staff might ask, 'What has come before?' In other words, what are the structures that have been previously drawn upon, and how have they been used? Structures become part of the store of knowledge that is available to the school leaders about interaction in the organisation, and while structures are re-produced (passed on) by various mechanisms, they can also be transformed or changed. Various structures may have served the school well in a past era, but these same structures may be the main causes of resistance to change at a time when the school has to adopt new practices or even to undertake a radical rethink of its purpose.

A typical strategic management task related to understanding a school's structuration may involve discovering answers to the following questions:

◆ What are the common 'myths' and 'legends' that are told to new staff during their informal induction?

◆ Who are the 'heroes and heroines' in the school and who were they if they have left?

◆ What events are remembered with humour or with reverence?

◆ Who are the 'change agents', the important people who lead change?

◆ What type of metaphors or symbolism is used in common day-to-day language to describe the school's processes, e.g., 'appraisal is about playing the game'; 'what date are we released from prison this term?'

◆ How do staff describe their school to others?

◆ What is acceptable behaviour: in the general staff meeting, in the principal's office, in front of students, at staff social events?

A school principal may involve staff in specific activities which develop strategic thinking. These activities might include: values scanning, detailing staff induction programmes, collecting staff histories, ethnographic studies of staff experiences, developing codes of conduct for the school, writing staff protocols on behaviour, developing influence charts, and redesigning staff organisational charts.

Critical Success Factors

A third strategy for developing strategic thinking skills is the use of 'critical success factors'. Herman and Herman (1995) suggest that critical success factors are those six to eight major responsibilities that are critical to the successful completion of an administrator's job. Thus, these factors are items that should determine the time spent and effort expended by the administrator. In our experience, very few schools have identified their critical success factors. This may help to explain why planning is ad hoc and reactive, rather than rational and proactive.

Critical success factors can be defined as those factors that provide an organisation with its best opportunities for achieving its mission and for ensuring that its mission is both relevant and consistent with the needs of its clients. Critical success factors are needed for review and evaluation – to determine if a programme or innovation can be expected to achieve its intended purpose within the organisation's values.

Critical success factors can be seen as 'macro' planning devices. They provide an overview for the whole organisation. Isolating critical success factors can be a way of both building strategic thinking and establishing a school management system. For example, the principal might ask senior staff to develop their critical success factors, which can then be used in the school's strategic plan and in staff development planning.

The main purpose of critical success factors, then, is to provide schools with information which helps them to determine whether they have been successful. Developing these factors is not an exact science, but thinking them through does offer some clear guidance about what is and is not important, and gives the school something against which to gauge success.

The following case shows how critical success factors were used by Mrs Lim to develop her teachers' strategic thinking:

■ | Mrs Lim made the following request at a general staff meeting: all staff were to develop a list of critical success factors for children entering their classes, but the list was not to include anything about academic standards. In other words, in the teachers' opinion, what should the children coming into their respective classes be able to do?

Initially the staff were taken aback by this request. They did not know where to start. While they were all good teachers and could easily describe the literacy standards that they would like students to have, they had a great deal of trouble thinking outside the bounds of their practice. Their experience of thinking strategically was indeed limited.

Mrs Lim herself decided to visit each teaching area and helped the staff to understand the task. After three months a number of critical success factors began to emerge, and by the end of the term all teachers had produced lists for their classes.

The following list is an example of one from a first grade primary teacher:

- Can the child's speech be understood by a policeman?
- Can the child be away from the parent all day without being upset?
- Can the child pay attention to a short story and answer questions about it?
- Can the child tie a knot with a bow?
- Can the child tell left from right?
- Can the child remember and carry out two or three tasks after being told once?
- Can the child put together a puzzle of six to twelve pieces?
- Can the child listen and then repeat a series of numbers accurately, such as 3-7-5-8-3?
- Can the child supply the last word to these phrases: mother is a woman and father is a ____; or fire is hot while ice cubes are ____?
- Can the child draw or copy a triangle?
- Can the child tell what time of the year Christmas occurs?
- Can the child tell what things are made of (chairs, shoes, etc.)?
- Does the child try to write or copy letters and numbers?

♦ Can the child explain what a T-shirt, shoes and hat have in common?

♦ Can the child easily admit that he or she does not know something or that help is needed?

At the conclusion of this task, when all the teachers had submitted their lists of critical success factors, Mrs Lim asked at another general meeting that the teachers share their lists. In this way, the teachers of grade 5 discussed with the teachers of grade 4 what they had seen as important in the students coming to them, and the teachers of grade 4 with the teachers of grade 3, and so on. The overall purpose of the session was to develop greater teamwork and understanding amongst the staff. ■

Teachers had started a process of defining what they valued from education and how they could achieve it. In the example, critical success factors were used to measure the success of children going into classes. They can also be used as a strategic exercise in a number of different ways. Staff, for example, could work out how the school's overall success should be measured. If such an exercise were to involve parents also, a list of critical success factors like the one below might emerge.

The things which determine our school's success are:

♦ we are able to offer the types of courses that the community wants, thus reducing the chances of falling enrolments;

♦ we use our community as a resource;

♦ we can develop business plans and budgets that enable the school to use resources more efficiently;

♦ we are able to build our image through an ongoing public relations programme;

♦ we build a culture of flexibility and an expectation of change; and

♦ we put a high priority on staff development.

While the exercise is obviously useful in reaching conclusions on what is important to the school and in setting some criteria against which success can be measured, it is also valuable in encouraging teachers and others to think about the school's performance in a strategic way.

Summary

Strategic plans are of little value if the people whose lives they impact are unable to think strategically. To use a sports metaphor, all the training undertaken by coaches and all the motivational activities used by the team psychologist will be to no avail unless the players are able to think strategically once they are on the field of play. We have provided some practical ways of building strategic thinking, including the use of three exercises: planning hexagons, critical operating tasks versus strategic management tasks, and critical success factors.

Finally, consider two schools that exist almost side by side. They are both government primary schools, built at a time when the suburbs they serviced were full of young families. Now, some fifteen years on, one school is thriving and has had to request extra staff and the placement of portable classrooms. It has huge community support and has an expanded programme of gymnastics, languages and music. Recently the minister has approved the building of a new air-conditioned gymnasium and sports complex. The other school is faced with closure, with enrolments shrinking rapidly and little community support.

Both schools have looked after their day-to-day operations with the same level of care. Neither has had any trouble worthy of note. The main difference is that the first school some time ago developed strategic thinking amongst its community by involving teachers and parents in planning how it might address an uncertain and difficult future, knowing that demographic changes were under way and that there were simply too few children in the area to support two institutions. The first school, through its strategic initiatives, sought to develop a deeper and more meaningful relationship with parents and to seek to understand how it might improve in the light of their expectations. It defined its uniqueness and the nature of its interaction with its environment. It positioned itself to take advantage of a complex situation. In contrast, the second school focused on maintenance, thought little about strategic direction and hoped that everything would turn out all right in the end.

Strategic thinking on the part of teachers and other stakeholders means an engagement with strategy. It means differentiating between the day-to-day issues of management and empowering people to question what should be, what could be and what is needed in order to achieve what is valued by the school.

CHAPTER 6

Values

We now explore why we believe a values-based approach to strategic planning is the right one for today's schools. We begin by defining what we mean by organisational values and the purposes they serve. Examples of different value statements are provided, and shifting societal values, espoused values, values-driven change and the content of value statements are all explained. To demonstrate the importance of values, a number of case studies of 'values in action' are presented and analysed. We also present some ideas on which values might drive schools of the future. We discuss values-driven schools and the role of principals and teachers in the process. We conclude with a warning: that schools must identify their values or they run the risk of becoming irrelevant to those whom they serve.

Values and Educational Administration

The term *values* is referred to often in organisations and throughout much of both Eastern and Western management literature of the 1990s. For example, in countries such as Singapore and Malaysia, we have seen a purposeful movement towards a rediscovery and reassertion of Asian values as the basis for societal and political action. Values have also recently become a major area of interest to educational administrators, again from both East and West (Begley, 1996). In Southeast Asia, for example, Bajunid (1996) promotes the need to clarify and articulate indigenous perspectives of educational management, particularly those values rooted in Islam. Similarly, Cheng and Wong (1996) have begun the search for cultural values and their influence on education in China, with a particular emphasis on Confucian values. In the Western context, researchers such as Begley (1996) and Leithwood (1992) describe the debate on the place of values in educational administration and their role in educational organisations.

There is a lively debate between those who believe that values play a key role in educational administration and those who work on the basis of scientific objectivity. The latter have a technical interest in educational administration and espouse a structural-rational perspective, in which positivist thought and scientific management predominate. For those who work within this paradigm, the organisation is considered to be a rationally designed instrument to serve the purposes of individuals or groups. It is assumed that decisions are based on rational analysis by drawing on scientifically valid knowledge. The organisation is seen as a structure of elements, each of which can be separately manipulated or modified without affecting the others in order to improve the efficiency of the whole. Thus, through the strategic plan, the organisation can be planned and controlled in line with explicit goals. For those who favour this approach to strategic planning, schematic diagrams and systems analyses are prevalent.

Using this approach, the administrator is able to stand outside the decision, and is able to remain personally detached and make value-free decisions based on what has been proven to be the best plan of 'management' (relationship 'laws' based on empirical-analytic knowledge) for attaining targets most efficiently and effectively. The contemporary parlance of this traditional organisational planning theory includes: teacher accountability, specified performance objectives, cost-benefit analysis, and performance indicators of teacher effectiveness.

For educational administrators who favour this approach, values have no place in management or in strategic planning. As Foster (1980) notes, such school principals would follow this traditional premise:

■ | To understand educational administration, one must acquire some sense of the development of administration generally.

> Modern administrative theory represents a transition from the art of politics and administration, where value judgements dominate, to a science of politics and administration, where value-free statements dominate. (p. 499) ∎

He adds:

> ∎ Values are neither incorrect nor correct and are of no concern to administrators. ∎

In other words, those business managers who follow this thinking simply deny that values have any role to play in planning. For them, charting the course of the business is about making hard business decisions. Reviews may lead to restructuring, which may in turn lead to retrenchments, but this is nothing to do with what the manager personally wants or likes. Managers have to be 'value-free'. Just as some physical scientists believe they cannot be held responsible for what their science is used for by politicians, so some business managers see business as a science.

A Cultural Approach

In contrast, a cultural perspective focuses on issues and concerns very different from those emphasised in traditional scientific organisational theory. Lakomski and Evers (1995) note:

> ∎ It is the cultural fabric of an organisation, in its many facets, that provides the only legitimate theoretical lens through which a social organisation such as a school can properly be described and its workings explained. (p. 10) ∎

Lakomski and Evers describe a more compelling understanding of contemporary organisations. This explanation suggests that principals cannot manage schools effectively without knowledge about and understanding of the values which underpin decisions and actions. Such an explanation appears to tie in with Greenfield's (1980, p. 38) interpretive or phenomenological view of organisations. To him, organisations are social creations. In order to understand organisations, we need to understand how intention becomes action and how intention and action on the part of some lead to intention and action by others. While it is easy to see how, from this perspective, we must conclude that people control organisations rather than the other way round, more recent evidence suggests that control is illusory. It would be more accurate to say that people 'influence' organisations, since such a view would accommodate the uncertainty of the environment. 'Control' suggests linearity of cause and effect, and that is more consistent with a rational, scientific model of organisations. The notion of influence, however, helps to explain the linkage between action and intent, and is consistent with the view that organisational actors are the ones who determine what might happen.

Hermeneutics argues that there is no absolute 'bottom line' upon which to justify knowledge claims and, hence, there is no possibility of certitude. What we come to accept as reasonable in terms of knowledge about our social and educational lives is the product of a socially and historically conditioned agreement. The rationality of that perspective is not, as it is for empiricism, that of abstract rules, instrumentalism, technical expertise and the criterion of prediction. On the contrary, hermeneutics poses a model of practical rationality that focuses on 'imagination, interpretation, the weighing of alternatives, and the application of criteria that are essentially open. Under a hermeneutic perspective there is no way of unambiguously determining right from wrong. Both the interpretation, and the extent to which we generally accept an interpretation, are practical matters of dialogue and discussion' (Smith and Blase, 1991, p. 11).

This is an essential element in breaking from traditional strategic planning. Traditional 'scientific' planning relies on the dispassionate neutral – perhaps a consultant – a 'value-free' person who can stand outside the organisation and make the 'right' decisions without the interference of personal links or involvement. It relies on the consultant selecting and applying parts and combinations of the various system theories in such a way that the plan would be considered of proven value. Value is proved through the use of: an environmental scan (identification of external influences and client need); an internal audit of current organisational programmes and their effectiveness (a review); an analysis of the gap or deficit between what the organisation should be doing and what it is doing (strategic direction analysis); and the application of scientific models of organisational problem solving, including mathematical models and systems analyses (what is 'best practice' in dealing with any deficit).

Strategic planning that is based on an interpretive perspective would be about collaborative dialogue and discussion to determine the appropriateness of decisions and actions. Such planning would either discard the consultant's role (a 'value-free' external person) altogether, or change the role to make it one of a reflective partner who is able to assist the organisation to see for itself its values and beliefs.

It would discard the need to begin with an environmental scan of external issues and client needs in favour of seeking clients' support in working together with staff to identify discursively what they believe the organisation exists to achieve. It would discard a 'scientific' audit of current programmes and productivity – a value-free external evaluation or review – in favour of seeking staff (and client) involvement in identifying practices that need to be kept or changed. It would discard objective gap analysis using scientific models. The key to planning, we argue, is not to search out deficits which must be rectified, but to seek an understanding of what the staff and community believe the organisation exists to achieve and to work out appropriate ways of making that happen. The key to planning is not 'value-free' prediction and control, but a building up from values of an understanding of how the organisation makes decisions and operates in an attempt to ensure that plans are based on structures – such as accepted practices, language and organisational culture – that are appropriate. Where it becomes apparent that existing structures need to be changed, the decision to change should come from a discursive and collaborative process of understanding, and should not be predicated by 'best practice' models from other contexts.

We feel we had to advance those arguments, even at the risk of distraction from the main practical purpose of our book, in order to establish the basis on which a values-based approach operates. If you are interested in pursuing some of the complex arguments surrounding values and educational administration, we refer you to Begley (1996), Chapman and Evers (1995) and Leithwood (1992), who provide commendable reviews of the state of the debate.

Defining Values

Hodgkinson (1978, p. 12), one of the most notable values theorists, defines a value as 'a conception, explicit or implicit, distinctive of an individual or characteristic of a group, of the desirable which influences the selection from available modes, means and ends of action'. Another renowned theorist, Thomas Greenfield (1986), suggests that values are springs of human action. Both theorists hold subjectivist notions that values are individual constructions of reality and that an observed 'shared social reality is a mosaic constructed from the building blocks of individual perception' (Begley, 1996, p. 411).

Other inquiries into values and educational administration have taken a more practical approach and investigated values and their relationship with administrative practices rather than their utility to philosophical debate (for examples see Begley and Leithwood, 1990; Campbell-Evans, 1993; Sergiovanni, 1995). In summarising this interest, Begley (1996, p. 412) suggests that the perspective has 'not so much denied an existence, as conceptually set (it) aside in favour of the firmer ground of collective social values and moral decision making. What becomes highlighted is the mainstream administrative domain of social accountability, consequence-focused, and/or consensus-based decision making'. Our interest in values as the driver of school planning is in line with this perspective.

Drawing on a more pragmatic perspective, Leithwood (1992) synthesises the work of others into values and defines them thus:

■ an enduring belief about the desirability of some means; and once internalised a value becomes a standard or criterion for guiding one's own actions and thought, for influencing the actions and thought of others, and for morally judging oneself and others. (p. 9) ■

In organisational terms, we see a school's shared or core values as the guidelines for action and, more specifically, for planning. Our approach to strategic planning is in line with Sergiovanni's (1995) broader conception of a values-based approach to school leadership. He states that the specification of beliefs and assumptions:

> ■ provides (schools) with a standard for determining what is good and bad, effective and ineffective, and acceptable and unacceptable. Using a values-based approach for defining the role of the principal not only ensures that what principals decide to do meets acceptable standards, but also provides the school with a set of indicators that defines its educational and moral health. (p. 7) ■

We believe the same basic philosophy holds true for school level strategic planning – that through clarifying shared values, schools prescribe *for themselves* acceptable standards and guides for decisions. As Burns (1978, p. 74) suggests, values 'indicate desirable and preferred end-states or collective goals or explicit purposes'. He then argues that values actually represent 'standards in terms of which specific criteria may be established and choices made among alternatives'. He even suggests that the term 'end values' describes values when they relate to goals and standards.

When we refer to values as the basis for planning and action, we are concerned about beliefs and the way of thinking about the 'life world' that enable an organisation to function. Values can be seen at the core of every decision made in organisations, and they are reflected in all structures and processes. Values anchor the operation of all organisations, whether they are commercial operations or public sector institutions like schools. The ways in which values are obtained can vary enormously, as can the awareness and linkage to broader, changing community values.

A shortcut to understanding operant values in the school is to ask on what basis a decision was made. Decisions are anchored in the values or theory of operation of the organisation. Some decisions may be counter to the organisation's values. Often, people may make decisions without being able to articulate their values. However, all decisions are anchored in values.

Figure 6.1 shows a definition of values as a theory of operation: the organisation's *raison d'être*. A theory of operation refers

Figure 6.1 Values: Theory of Operation

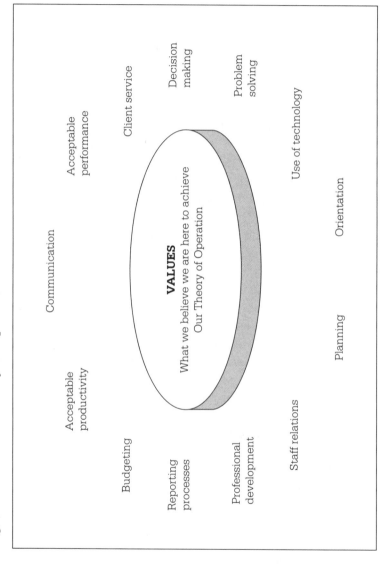

to what members believe their organisation's purpose is. It also incorporates the principles they follow in order to achieve the purpose. Values anchor all aspects of operation, as shown in the figure: how planning is approached and driven; acceptable ways of communicating; acceptable levels of performance; and issues such as staff access to resources.

The way in which a school is structured and how it operates is dependent upon its value system. As Schon (1990) writes:

> ■ Value systems correspond to, and are inseparable from, theory. Within the theory of an industrial firm, there are values related to the maintenance of profit margins, share of market, quality of product, reduction in cost of operations, and satisfying the stockholders. And there may be informal values related to the culture of the company – for example, values placed on smooth relations between people, life tenure for employees, and minimal contact with outsiders. (p. 25) ■

In some cases, while values are not explicitly laid out, they can be read from the way in which things work. Take, for example, the recent move by education systems throughout the world towards greater autonomy for schools. This move reflects a shift in values. How it was derived and how it may be interpreted by various groups may differ. Some claim such a move can disadvantage schools in lower socio-economic areas, but others may see it as a justifiable way to rationalise costs and to increase accountability. Regardless of how it is interpreted, the move represents a clear change in the values that determine what is acceptable and unacceptable practice in schools – in Schon's language, it is 'theory of operation'. It represents a cultural shift. Such moves would have been rejected only a short time ago, when equality of educational provision was of paramount importance in people's minds. Such shifts in system values are accompanied by parallel changes in community values. It is of no surprise, therefore, that education systems are perceived to be driven almost solely by economic considerations.

Values-driven Schools

Sergiovanni makes a case for values-driven schools by holding that, once schools have developed common and shared values, these should become the 'compass points' for guiding the school's formal and informal operation; 'that shared values provide the "glue" that bonds people together in a loosely connected world' (Sergiovanni, 1995, p. 55). In other words, the development of shared or core values is the basis for what school communities do. The development of shared values or understandings helps members of the school community to categorise common meanings and so facilitate organisational communication and organisational perceptions. Put together, these provide a certain cohesion and identity for creating a 'unifying moral order from which teachers and students derive direction, meaning and significance' (Sergiovanni, 1995, p. 132).

Our approach to strategic planning suggests a structure for determining and clarifying core values. This is the first and the most important stage of the planning process. As Patterson states, 'any attempt then at innovation or development planning should begin with the school clarifying its core values' (1993, p. 31). He adds:

> Whether we are in the hardware business or the school business, we can't create a preferred future without knowing what we stand for. So many organisations try to be all things to all people and end up being nothing to anyone. They become driven by events, flitting from one innovation to another in search of the magic box that, once installed, will never have to be unplugged again. In schools, the magic box can take the form of mastery learning, Management by Objectives, Total Quality Management, outcome-based education, transformational leadership, and on and on. (p. 39)

There is nothing inherently wrong with many of the innovations which have been directed at schools, but they may have little utility if they are at variance with prevailing values or needs. Reacting to events too may limit our capacity to influence our future.

A natural starting point for developing a values-driven approach to planning is a willingness to accept and learn from the multiplicity of values which exist in the school's community. We know there are differences in values. Leadership involves an understanding of the personal realities which are constructed by individuals (Whiteley, 1995). Instead of one set of imposed corporate values, it is the shared, contested vision and values which become the foundation stones of organisations that learn (Senge, 1990). As Starratt (1993, p. 15) notes, leadership is often described as though leaders and followers inhabit the same, uniform meaning-world, but in reality the world is a place in which meaning is something always to be negotiated, and in a multi-cultural and multi-class society we cannot assume that leaders and subordinates agree on what things mean – in other words, they have different values (also see Tierney, 1996).

Through understanding the importance of values in strategic planning, school leaders learn to understand more deeply the multiple contexts within which students learn and teachers teach. To reject values is to deny the uniqueness of individual students, teachers and other members of the school's community. An acceptance of the critical importance of values denotes the contribution which diversity makes to organisational improvement.

If schools are to change and work positively with their diverse communities, values should become one of their prime foci for planning. School leaders must, in Angus's (1989, p. 84) words, 'penetrate the level of immediacy of everyday action and consider the practices of schooling in relation to the social, cultural, political and economic context of education'.

Traditional Organisational Values

It is insufficient for a school's leadership to state that there are clear, desirable or universal values to which the school must adhere. Planning for school improvement, we argue, must be based on the premise that schools have different values and that these values must be mapped before strategic intent can be determined.

Of course, one may argue that there are such things as universal values, and this is an argument developed by Beck (1993), who contends that values are objective and that some values are universally considered more important than others. For example, it is more than likely that most schools would value equity of access to education and that all children should have the opportunity to develop to their fullest potential. Such values are indeed intensely compelling.

Along the same lines, schools with traditional values may be seen as places where people work in harmony towards the same ends and produce academically able students. This view is consistent with the view of organisations as machines, characterised by predictability, rationality and control. Operation is driven by the values of dominant cultural groups, which often ignore cultural values important to individual communities (Walker and Quong, 1998, in press). As Villa and Thousand (1995) suggest:

> they (schools) are attempting to provide an excellent education for the elite, Americanize new immigrant populations, and otherwise track children for stratified work roles in a relatively static factory economy in which query, creative problem solving, and collaboration are not wanted or needed ... school communities unconsciously (or consciously) still attempt to promote a common, homogeneous culture (i.e., the white, Anglo-Saxon, Protestant, rural culture of the 1800s). (p. 31) ■

Such values are easily seen in classrooms in teacher-centred and traditional ways of teaching, curriculum and school structures. Teaching, for example, is guided by ingrained understandings of what a teacher 'is', how students learn within the classroom and what teacher-student relationships *should* look like. Such traditional values bases, anchoring both formal and informal behaviours in classrooms, have honoured comfort, conformity, efficiency and order above all else (Walker and Walker, 1998, in press).

Traditional values in schools unavoidably influence, and are influenced by, the shape of leadership. The values and beliefs apparent in school structures, community and learning approaches often remain rooted in inflexible functionalist principles which encourage an overemphasis on the rational–technical aspects of leadership at the expense of non-rational elements (Begley, 1996; Burrell and Morgan, 1979). Leadership guided by such beliefs holds that better school practices can best be discovered by a search for measurable facts (Macpherson, 1996). The uncritical acceptance of such facts often guides leaders towards a dispassionate focus on measurable aspects of inputs, outputs and processes, and to view school life as characterised by underlying patterns of logic, system and order.

When such values direct leadership practices, leaders tend not to search for particular needs in organisations but, instead, try to identify patterns of similarity between people and how people make links. Links are based on what staff have in common: their sameness. Once patterns of sameness are identified, they are used as the basis for controlling the work environment. Different values are seen as disruptive and are therefore largely ignored. From the traditional perspective, people with different values are not seen as team players.

Capturing and collecting individual values involve a shift in the role of the leader. Many leaders have been socialised to believe that an organisation is weak if people openly express views that conflict with organisational directives. Walker (1994) summarises this perspective thus:

■ Some managers insist that the best way to reduce conflict and maintain harmony is to focus on the ways in which people (and structures) are alike. It is argued that people work together best if they ignore their differences. (p. 214) ■

Pursuing this line, leaders recruit staff and encourage early socialisation mechanisms which provide them with people who 'fit the mould' and who cause as little disturbance as possible (Patterson, 1993). When differences emerge, for the sake of superficial harmony leaders ignore them by playing on similarities, using clichés like 'We're all in it for the kids'. In the desire for comfort and efficiency, school leadership often remains at a management level and avoids respecting individual values, since opening up different perspectives would intensify the anxiety provoked by conflict. Sergiovanni (1995, p. 95), though, points out that not all schools with strong cultures are characterised by harmony. Indeed, value conflicts, well mediated, are at the core of any strong school culture. Managing cultural diversity, and balancing and valuing the different values of the staff and community are the keys to strong leadership.

A diversity of values may be seen as an essential ingredient which will help modern organisations to be flexible and to learn. They need to do these things in order to meet the constantly changing demands placed on them by their communities and clients.

Patterson (1993) suggests that, for schools to change to meet new demands, they should be driven by values that are different from those which have traditionally framed education. In Table 6.1, he provides a list of values that he believes should drive schools of the future. He contrasts these with the espoused values which typify today's schools.

While schools are driven or influenced by values and assumptions which do not differentiate cultural beliefs, individual contexts or future needs, and which assume generalised ways of working, it may be questioned whether schools are meeting the needs of their communities. This inevitably leads us to consider *whose* values have traditionally driven schools.

Global Issues: Whose Values?

The values driving many schools often trivialise or even ignore cultural and localised needs and beliefs. In many ways, traditional values have stemmed not from schools but from values external to the school. Such values have often ignored cultural and community values, and have emanated from economic, culturally restricted and expert-defined beliefs about schools. Examples abound. In Hong Kong, for example, the adoption several years ago of an approach to school-based management (labelled the School Management Initiative), basically developed in Australia, exemplified an innovation based on values that were incompatible with the context. There are many present-day examples of systems seeking to import initiatives and practices which are driven by values that may be incongruent with their own. For instance, some education systems in the West have been attracted by academic performance in certain Asian systems and have believed – in some cases, with the support of eminent academics – that such initiatives could be imported wholesale.

Ironically, the flow of influence is also going in the opposite direction. In several Asian states, for example, foreign educational initiatives and accompanying values are sometimes imported without a due consideration of culture. There is even a quaint belief in some systems that 'West is best', which serves merely to pull policy and practice towards global sameness.

Table 6.1 Today's and Tomorrow's Values

Value One: Openness to Participation

Today's Value: Our organisation values employees listening to the organisation's leaders and doing what the leaders tell them to do.	Tomorrow's Value: Our organisation values employees actively participating in any discussion or decision affecting them.

Value Two: Openness to Diversity

Today's Value: Our organisation values employees falling in line with the overall organisational direction.	Tomorrow's Value: Our organisation values diversity in perspective leading to a deeper understanding of organisational reality and an enriched knowledge base for decision making.

Value Three: Openness to Conflict

Today's Value: Our organisation values employees communicating a climate of group harmony and happiness.	Tomorrow's Value: Our organisation values resolving conflict in a healthy way that leads to stronger solutions of complex issues.

Value Four: Openness to Reflection

Today's Value: Our organisation values employees conveying a climate of decisiveness. Firm decisions are made and implemented without looking back.	Tomorrow's Value: Our organisation values employees reflecting on their own and others' thinking in order to achieve better organisational decisions.

Value Five: Openness to Mistakes

Today's Value: Our organisation values employees concentrating on making no mistakes and working as efficiently as possible.	Tomorrow's Value: Our organisation values acknowledging mistakes and learning from them.

Source: Patterson (1993, pp. 1–14).

Policy makers and practitioners tend to ignore the significance of culture in the formulation and adoption of educational policy and its implementation in practice (see Hallinger and Leithwood, 1996). Culture is often ignored, with the 'same' policies and practices being accepted regardless of cultural 'difference'. This reflects a mindset that is symbolised by such expressions as 'if it works for them, it will work for us', 'why reinvent the wheel?' and the so-called quality notion that what is 'best practice' for someone else must also be 'best practice' for us.

Given the significance of culture (Angus, 1995; Hargreaves, 1994), it is surprising that much of the current literature and practice in educational leadership and policy making appears to ignore it. For example, standard texts in the field of educational administration draw almost exclusively on perspectives taken from Western literature and practice. These paradigms tend to be adopted uncritically and unquestioningly by academics and practitioners in societies, schools and cultures which bear little similarity to those in which the theories originated (Hofstede, 1994). This situation is compounded by the fact that many such theories and perspectives are generated in the corporate business sector and then unthinkingly transferred and applied to education (e.g., Martinsons, 1996; Radford, Mann, Ohta and Nakane, 1993). The overbearing Western influence on management thinking results in a powerful pull towards the same values both within and between societies (see, for example, Walker, Bridges and Chan, 1996).

A further manifestation of the cultural 'values' pull arises from the trend towards globalisation of education, which has, in turn, promoted the phenomenon of 'sameness', or what can be labelled 'cultural borrowing'. This can be illustrated by the global push over the past decade towards decentralisation and school-based management. Policy makers in countries with contrasting cultures have tended to follow similar policy blueprints to those adopted by many Western governments that, for diverse reasons, have chosen to restructure the administrative structures and processes of their public sectors. This phenomenon, also called 'policy cloning', permeates both strategic and operational policy and school planning (Dimmock and Walker, 1998, in press). Questions naturally arise about the relevance, applicability, validity and appropriateness of theories, perspectives and policies which are transferred to, or borrowed, adopted and 'cloned' by, education systems whose cultures and situational conditions are quite dissimilar from those in which they were conceived.

Top-down Imposition of Values to Drive Change

The question of whose values have traditionally driven school operation can be addressed also from a leadership perspective. The recent emphasis on schools developing 'mission' and 'vision' has raised an expectation that leaders should be visionaries with the wisdom to articulate vision and the charisma to carry it through.

The top-down imposition of values in schools mirrors prevalent approaches in Western business. In some commercial operations, values have been seen as important, and so management has designed the values that it supposes would be useful, and has then set about making sure that all employees learn to believe in these values. Values may be consciously developed by senior management as a vehicle for changing, saving or redirecting the organisation for a specific purpose.

As an example, take the following statement from the CEO of an international Australian company, Austrade, which employs over 600 people. Langhorne (1992) says of the CEO's moves to restructure the company:

> ■ | The new management team decided very early that Austrade would be a values-driven organisation. Values were agreed upon and are now being driven hard by management at all levels throughout the organisation. (p. 19) ■

In Austrade, the values were deliberately selected by management as the basis for organisational restructuring. Importantly, these values were determined by senior management only, a set of 'designer values'. To Langhorne, the values-driven approach is where specific values are adopted by management, imposed on staff, and then used as a basis and justification for major changes of process and structure within the organisation.

Smyth (1989) would argue that such an approach is highly problematic. He suggests that, while it is vital that leaders have the ability to empower people to make them feel stronger and in control of their own destinies, this cannot be done by simply imposing values from above. Successful leaders are not simply leaders who exude power and confidence, but they empower others by creating an exciting, stimulating environment in which others feel motivated to contribute. This, for us, is the essence of leadership: a role which enables all organisational members and stakeholders to have a part to play in developing values which drive planning and change.

Shared Values

In values based strategic planning, school vision and values should be identified and clarified largely by the school community itself. In his landmark work *The Fifth Discipline: The Art and Practice of the Learning Organization*, Senge (1990) criticises the 'top-down' view and urges organisations to develop a 'shared vision' or, in our terms, shared or core values. Senge first calls on organisations to build a shared vision by rejecting the idea that a vision must come from on high. He suggests that, problematically, in most organisations, vision does not result from building on people's personal values but reflects only the strategic or official vision as developed by one or two people. If vision is developed in such a manner, claims Senge, 'there is little opportunity for inquiry and testing at every level so that people feel they understand and own vision' (p. 216). As a result, the 'official' vision fails to foster energy and commitment.

Rost (1991) agrees with Senge's assertions, while calling for leaders and followers to develop mutual purpose. Lieberman and Miller (1990) too suggest that successful school improvement efforts depend on reaching into the invisible aspects of school life and on tapping the energy and commitment of teachers.

Developing a shared understanding is a common theme in much of the literature. Senge (1990) neatly summarises the importance of developing a shared vision:

> When you add up the pieces of the hologram (individual values) the image of the whole does not change fundamentally. After

all, it was there in each piece. Rather the image becomes more intense, more lifelike. When more people come to share a common vision, the vision may not change fundamentally. But it becomes more alive, more real in the sense of the mental realism that people truly imagine achieving. (p. 213) ■

Hutchinson and Whitehouse (1986) offer a dissenting view in suggesting that educators uncritically accept the social reality in which they are immersed and within which certain role models are accepted unconditionally. In our experience, however, teachers and administrators are conscious of their reality, but they may be seen as uncritically accepting because they have traditionally not had the opportunity to express their values. Because of this lack of voice, they have felt disempowered and unable to contribute, which, in turn, has provoked frustration and uncertainty. Essentially, the mistake is in believing that, because dissent is not voiced, it is not there. It is probably suppressed in a far more dangerous form below the surface.

Many teachers, if given the opportunity, will try to express the incongruity between their own values and the social reality of their school, and this is the strength of a values based strategic plan. Teachers, managers and relevant others will indeed involve themselves when given the opportunity and will, through a process of challenging existing values, piece together the hologram to form an acceptable school reality.

If we look specifically at planning, historically, school level actors have been given very little say in decisions relating to major educational change and have been faced by its seemingly endless contradictions. When schools were not asked to produce long-term strategic plans, teachers (and often principals) were rarely consulted about the school's direction or asked to express opinions about the relevance of what they were teaching to what was valued by their community. Moves towards self-managing schools and an emphasis on school improvement, quality, effectiveness and efficiency may provide a window of opportunity for teachers to overcome the tensions created by these contradictions. Through involvement in strategic planning, teachers have the opportunity to ensure that the values they hold can drive the processes, curriculum and structures in their institutions.

It is important to stress that developing shared values does not act to restrict innovation at an individual level; rather, the process serves to guide decision making and action in the school. Sergiovanni (1995, p. 55) emphasises that 'specific goals and purposes remain the responsibility of teachers and others to decide as long as they embody the values'. He goes on to say 'that everyone is free to do the things that make sense to them providing the decisions they make about what to do embody the values that are shared' (p. 134).

We now move on to discuss a number of key issues related to values-based planning. The first of these is the paradox between espoused values and operant values. The second issue relates to the form which core values take and how they are developed. Dealt with inappropriately, their ability to influence school life is seriously impaired. Third, we look at the issue of school values versus system requirements or societal values.

Espoused Values

Consider the following statement made when the principal of a public sector school was asked about his school's values:

> ■ 'In this school, we maintain that all of our decisions, our pro-
> grammes and actions can be held accountable to the following
> values. When we make a decision, or embark on an educational
> programme or activity, it will be because:
>
> ◆ it will really make a difference to the education of students;
> or
>
> ◆ it will really make a difference to the chances of students
> getting jobs; or
>
> ◆ it supports teachers' professional development and well-
> being; and
>
> ◆ it is an 'open' decision, made with no secrets being kept
> from parents or students; and
>
> ◆ it has involved administration in actively seeking the input
> of staff'. ■

This list sounded very impressive and indicated that the principal had certainly paid much attention to the values of the school, but when asked if he believed that these values had been useful in planning, he became somewhat sceptical. He said:

■ 'It's all very well to conjecture about this stuff, but really, when it comes down to it, the department won't have anything of it. After all, someone has to be responsible, and, in the department's view, that someone is me, the principal'. ■

Values like 'really making a difference to students' education' are nice for teachers to theorise about, but in the harsh reality of schools, decisions are made for the greater good of the running of the whole school, and this often means that some of the decisions are educationally unsound. Handed down from the centre, they are clearly economic and have little to do with ideals about education.

The fact that an organisation has a publicly stated set of values is no guarantee that these are the values that drive its operations and actions. Many organisations have a visible set of values which they openly espouse, but, too often, these are not reflected in practice. In the above example, while the school had developed a set of value statements, it was clear that the principal did not believe in them and did not feel able to put them into practice.

Thus, we have a situation in many institutions where the rhetoric is at variance with the reality. A school, for example, that claims publicly to care about students as individuals may initially attract people who are searching for this type of environment. If, however, the actual practice of the school revolves around teaching all students of a certain age exactly the same thing using singular teaching methodologies, people will soon realise the espoused values are little more than hollow words. This can have adverse consequences. Disillusionment can easily lead to a withdrawal of support.

A further example serves to emphasise the point. A principal in a primary school had just completed a further degree in School Management and Development. She was excited about what she had learned about professional development and how it might help teachers. In her first week back at school, she gathered the staff together and addressed them, reading from a short statement she had prepared for the teachers' handbook and the parents' newsletter. In her speech she said:

> ■ 'I believe that it is very important we all learn and develop continuously throughout our careers. To learn, we must take risks, learn to experiment together and take advantage of learning opportunities which are available both in and outside the school ... I would like you all to think about what you can do to further your development'. ■

Teachers thought this was a very positive move. Many had previously felt that their further development had not been a priority. Mr Wong and Miss Lim went away and talked about how they could take advantage of what the principal had said. They decided that some team teaching would be a good way of learning from each other. Another teacher, Mr Shapra, had been wanting to upgrade his computer skills for some time and identified a two-day course organised by the Ministry of Education. The three teachers wrote their development plans and submitted them optimistically to the principal. Approximately one week later, she called them into her office and, much to their surprise, rejected both of their proposals. She explained that there was no way she could reorganise the timetable to allow team teaching or peer observation and, anyway, doubted that such an approach would be of much benefit. She told Mr Shapra that the school could not spare him for two days, nor would it be able to pay the course fees. She suggested that he work on his computer skills at home. Needless to say, the teachers left the office dejected and had serious doubts about whether the principal meant even a word of what she had said at the meeting a week earlier. While she had outlined one set of values about professional development, her real values were evident through her actions.

This common problem of a gap between rhetoric and reality may be the result of how the values were derived. As we said earlier, in many organisations, values are formulated by a select group of top managers, sometimes with the help of expert outsiders. Vision and mission statements are written, sometimes with some accompanying material about values. These statements usually represent the views of the chief and they are then handed down the line for people to accept. They are presented as something which describes the whole organisation, even though the vast majority of organisational members have little or no involvement in the process.

Many schools, particularly in the 1980s, led by harassed and overworked principals, were expected to come up with statements about values and direction, and it was usually the individual at the top who had to do it. It was the 'in' thing to do. Large business operations were doing it, so why couldn't schools? Statements were incorporated into handbooks, prospectuses, newsletters and the like, but the outcome of all this was something which the school simply could not live up to. It looked impressive, but it was largely worthless.

What Are Values and How Do They Affect Schools?

Given all that we have discussed to this point, especially in relation to the subjective nature of values and the fact that true values can only be developed collaboratively in context (by people in real school settings), it is not possible for us to produce an example of 'good' school values in action. As we noted in relation to Patterson's list of values, such lists support the objective view that some values are more important than others. We have argued that cultural differences make this assumption highly problematic.

It is appropriate that we should describe what impact values have on school life, and to do this, we draw on a couple of examples from our own experience. The first describes a clash of values and comments on the dynamic nature of values: how they reflect the beliefs of people in the organisation. The second looks at how specifically expressed values can serve to guide decisions and actions, and how, in one particular case, they can be used as part of a personnel selection process.

Case 1: A Values Clash

Wong Ngai Leung was employed by the Hong Kong Department of Education for eighteen years. He was a teacher, department head and assistant principal. Based on his experience and qualifications, he applied for and was successful in gaining a position in the central office as a curriculum advisor.

Mr Wong valued a highly structured environment where all activities were clearly defined and well documented, with little scope for flexible or creative work practices. He was someone who liked things done properly and on time.

The unit that he joined, however, valued flexibility, individual creativity and initiative. The unit provided services that supported teachers and department policy implementation. This often meant dropping everything to work as a team in response to an immediate policy change or directive from the senior management group. The office also worked with less administrative support staff than some would have thought necessary for the tasks it had to perform. As a result, some bureaucratic 'shortcuts' had become standard practices. They were, of course, a contravention of office protocols, but without them, advisors would rarely get out into schools.

Not surprisingly, Mr Wong did not fit in very well. Imagine what it would be like working with him if you had been used to a flexible environment. You might question why Mr Wong wanted the job in the first place and then why he was given it. Perhaps the values which anchored the work of the advisory team had never been delineated. Even if they were, they had not been used in selection. There were two possible outcomes to this episode: either there would be a shift of values to reflect the values positions of those employed in the unit, including Mr Wong; or he would find working with the others too uncomfortable and would want to leave.

This example serves to demonstrate how values are important in decision making. You will notice that we talked about the possibility of a shift in values. They are not static. They may change as people flow in and out of the organisation.

Case 2: Expressed Values Guide Decisions

Another issue which emerges from our discussion of values is that of form and specificity. Arguably, the greater the degree of specificity, the greater the likelihood that they can determine decision choices. As an example of this, consider the following values taken from the Northern Territory School Principals' Association in Australia. These specific values, it is claimed, guide all the association's decisions and actions:

Networking	We will shape the national educational agenda through our contributions made as part of the national network of educational leaders.
Recognition	We will maintain a high educational and political profile with recognition from the wider educational community.
Support	We will support our members: personally, professionally, industrially and politically. Recognition of members' expertise and experience will be actively promoted.
Professional Development	We acknowledge the essential leadership role of principals and actively promote, provide and encourage the development of best practice.
Diversity	We value and encourage the individual differences of our members, recognising that through diversity will come best practice.
Participation	We will be actively involved in community issues and educational political debate, to enhance quality education.
Integrity	We demand ethical behaviour from all our members. This behaviour is defined by our Code of Ethics, accepted protocols and constitution.
Equity	We actively promote equal opportunities for support and development for all of our members regardless of: location, gender, race, or any form of handicap or disability.

These value statements supposedly provide the association with what they consider values specific enough to be used to anchor their decisions. For example, if the association's executive officer makes a serious decision that is questioned after the event by the members of the association, he or she should be able to show how the decision fulfils one or more of the values.

Recently, the Principals' Association received a grant from the government to engage a new full-time executive officer. They decided that the person to fill the position need not be an experienced principal, or even a professional educator, but that the person *must* meet the essential values of the organisation. In the selection process, the panel asked each applicant to read through a case study and then to describe how he or she would respond. The panel then assessed the applicants against the values they espoused. In the knowledge that the applicants' descriptions of what they would do may not have been how they would respond in reality, the selection panel also quizzed the applicants' referees about what they had observed of the applicants' values in action.

Value statements must be specific enough to guide schools' operation, decision making and planning. Loose statements expressing little more than effusive platitudes do little for building shared and common understandings and values. The importance of values, of course, is not simply how they are defined or written. Of greater importance are the reasons for an organisation choosing to emphasise its values.

Values and Student Socialisation

Understanding values in the school context is probably more important than in any other organisational situation. Why? The answer lies in the fact that part of the school's remit includes teaching values to students.

Educators often overlook that one of the main purposes of schools is to socialise children. Immersing them in the values and beliefs of their culture and community is an important role of schools. What schools do, how they are structured, standards of acceptable dress and behaviour, the myths and stories they tell, and the heroes and heroines they idolise are all part of what the school is and as such are an integral part of any process of change. They must therefore form part of any strategic plan.

Many schools believe that their overriding purpose is to get their students successfully through the examination system. Such schools, for example, might project the following beliefs:

◆ Our goal is to increase the participation rate of students to year 12; or

◆ Our purpose is to increase the number of students who achieve better than five passes in the final examinations.

As Codd (1984) points out, such schools serve to reproduce certain types of social values and act to reinforce the existing social structure in our community:

■ Firstly, the conviction that competition is necessary and desirable is important to the legitimisation of a 'free-market' economy. Indeed such a political economy could not survive without a common commitment to this belief. Thus examinations and tests are part of a tangible system of rewards and inducements by which students are thought to be motivated to compete. Secondly, the conviction that individual achievement is the result of ability combined with effort is fundamental to the meritocratic ideal that legitimates the allocation of individuals within a hierarchy of opportunities, status and rewards. (p. 21) ■

We do not disagree that the purpose of schools is to reproduce the values of the society that they serve. This may be both unavoidable and desirable. Our contention is that schools need to ensure that the values they are reproducing do in fact cohere with the social values of their community, that they are not simply 'hangovers' from a previous time, which are no longer relevant, or, worse, are the imposed values of a system of education that has never been aligned with the community's needs.

Consider a school in an isolated Aboriginal community in Australia. Strict adherence to a centralised curriculum taught by teachers who have come from large urban cities may very easily fail to reproduce the values of the community they serve in favour of a generic set of community values. Equally, a school located in Malaysia that operates largely according to Western educational values, which are incongruent with local indigenous values, may not be addressing its own contextual needs.

Consider also the changing nature of contemporary employment patterns. Gone is any expectation that when you start work after leaving school you will still be with that first employer when you retire. The value traditionally placed on lifelong tenure or on having only one type of job or career throughout a working life is all but gone. Values-driven schools recognise that training students for single careers that exist today is to blind those they serve to the fact that those careers may not exist in even the short-term future. Equipping them for lifelong learning has become the catch cry of most futurists.

Schools should consciously strive to identify the values they are reproducing. The current emphasis on strategic planning or action creates an ideal environment in which values identification can occur. A school cannot take for granted that its desired outcomes will serve to convey the values commonly held in the school community, especially if these values are unknown or unidentified.

Too often, strategic planning in schools does not take values into account, because, as we have already said in previous chapters, planning is pursued commonly through a top-down approach. Such an approach is dominated by values which the key individuals see as vital for systemic conformity, even though in many cases the individuals concerned may personally disagree with such espoused values. An essential element of strategic planning in self-managing schools is that administrators have the freedom to explore the contradiction between their personal (and professional) values and their perceptions of social reality. This process of joint exploration is essential if the purposes and activities of the school are to stay true to the wants and needs of the school's community.

An example of the pitfalls of traditional top-down planning may reinforce our point:

■ A college (catering for 16 to 18-year-olds) recently restructured and developed a strategic plan through a top-down approach. The plan was developed by a committee led (and dominated) by the principal and senior managers. The plan proposed that the college should continue to hold an annual sports day. This tradition had been established in the college some twenty years earlier when it was a comprehensive high school (years 8–12). Most staff believed that the event no longer served a valid purpose and consumed large amounts of time and other resources which could be better used to assist underachieving students. Most students anyway did not attend the event, using the time instead to stay at home. Nevertheless, the plan set the budget and staffing for the event for the next five years. Even the principal saw little point in holding the sports day but was reluctant to be the one to break with tradition. ■

Such an approach did not serve the college's interests well. The intention of strategic planning is to develop an open atmosphere that facilitates the exploration and examination of the community's own values and beliefs. Such an examination aims to generate contradictions between what the school community believes in and what is espoused through the current function and structure of the institution. It is through these contradictions that the principal can develop meaningful objectives (which can be subjected to critical scrutiny) that form the basis for the school's strategic plan. In this way, the principal can become more innovative and less submissive to tradition.

School administrators need to become more knowledgeable about the ways in which teachers, students and other members of the community become part of the system of social and cultural reproduction. As Giroux (1983) notes:

> ■ Bourdieu argues that the school and other social institutions legitimate and reinforce, through specific sets of practices and discourses, class-based systems of behaviour and dispositions that function to reproduce the existing dominant society ... the notion of learning in which a child internalises the cultural messages of the school not only via the latter's official discourse (symbolic mastery), but also through the messages embodied in the 'insignificant' practices of daily classroom life. (p. 32) ■

The values and behaviours that society wishes to be legitimated through the school system are first demanded by the administration of its teaching staff. Traditional management, therefore, incorporates practices such as:

- ◆ rigidly scheduled staff meetings regardless of necessity;
- ◆ dress regulations for teachers;
- ◆ strict adherence to programming format and schedules;
- ◆ extra duties such as sports teams after school;
- ◆ teacher 'sign-on' attendance boards; and
- ◆ inspectors who judge teacher performance.

In the same way that cultural practices and norms are reproduced through the classroom, the management practices of school administration can also be said to reproduce social norms in the teaching staff. Successful strategic planning must include activities that expose these 'legitimating' administrative practices in order to enable teachers, administrators and other educators to view them not as immutable, but as practices to be challenged when developing plans.

To recap, we have examined the role of schools in reproducing our society. We have noted that values identification is even more important in schools than in other organisations. We have warned that while all schools may have goals, philosophies or aims that reflect their values, many schools' intentions are based on inappropriate values which have not been formulated by those who are part of the school's context. Some schools may be reproducing inappropriate values because the values of the community they serve have changed. A question which naturally arises from such a discussion is: are schools really isolated from the influence of the imposed values of central authorities? We shall now attempt to address this important issue.

School Values and Central Requirements

Up to this point, we have assumed that schools have the scope to develop their own value statements. However, few schools are completely independent of the influence of central governments or employing bodies. Consider a school, for example, which has been set up by the government in a rural community, where the curriculum and purpose of the central government's school education system is in conflict with the values of the community the school is there to service. This is not an infrequent occurrence. You may be familiar with the scenario of a community in which education for girls is seen as inessential, yet the school is established to make equal provision for boys and girls. In such a case, the school sets out to change the values of the community it is there to serve.

It is important in values based strategic planning to recognise the place of imposed values, directions and guidelines. Schools are not isolated from such influences. Rather, school value systems are an amalgam of the values that are imposed and the values that stem from the school's personnel and community.

To explain this view, we have adapted Mintzberg's (1994) model of planning influence (see Figure 6.2). In this model the arrow marked 'External Directions, Policies and Procedures' indicates those direct influences from the central authority and other external bodies that impact on the school. They can, for example, be direct instructions in the form of codes of conduct, by-laws, regulations, employment instructions and directives that the school is compelled to follow, or they can be suggested procedures such as are found in departmental school handbooks.

External influences can also be from other bodies besides ministries and governing bodies. The impact of church groups on curriculum (such as the teaching of evolution or sex education), of direct government intervention, or of social censorship (banned books, banned speakers, and so forth) can be considerable.

The smaller arrows marked 'Selected Directives' and 'Unrealized Strategy' acknowledge that few schools can be said to follow all the rules to the letter of the law. In many cases, the

Figure 6.2   Values: Strategic Conflict

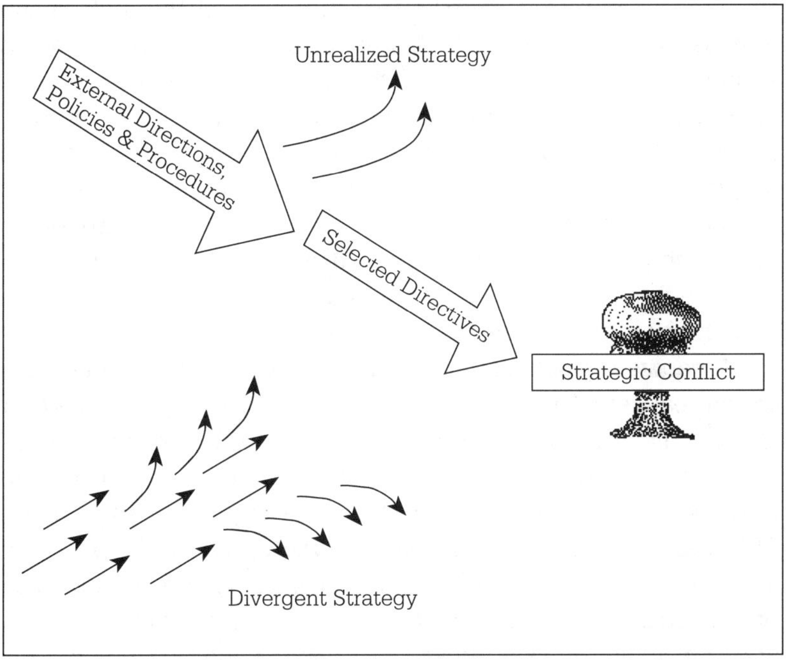

school will make conscious or unstated decisions to ignore certain external regulations or parts of them in order to effect the smooth running of operations and for better community relations. For instance, where a central authority has directed that the staff of all schools in the region must be at school until 4 p.m., the schools may decide to allow a more flexible work practice in order to promote goodwill and to encourage the support of teachers for certain events out of school hours. Another example may be where a directive from the department prohibits the use of untrained personnel, but where schools choose to use parents to help out in classrooms, a practice which is seen as being in the best interests of children and teachers.

In democratic nations, the overall impact of external influences on the values that anchor the decisions made in schools is slight in comparison to the impact of the values that the staff and students bring to the school daily. This is particularly so in those countries where schools are predominantly self-managing, with the result that the external directives from central authorities are gradually lessening.

We have looked at the impact of external directives and strategies. Now let us turn to the strategies of the staff in the organisation. Mintzberg (1994) advances the notion of 'emergent strategies'. He suggests that staff will pull together and that coming out of this collaboration is an accepted 'strategy' or 'way of doing'. Mintzberg's idea may be somewhat simplistic. Teachers may collaborate in such ways as to give rise to emergent coherent strategies, but not by chance. What can and does happen in many schools is that the Balkanised nature of teaching, which sees teachers in closed classrooms and closed faculties, means that their strategies are often divergent rather than emergent.

A secondary school, for example, may have five social education teachers. One may have been trained in England, another in Australia, and yet another in the USA. While each of these teachers may be directed by the government to teach a centralised social education syllabus, the pedagogy is left up to them. The strategies they adopt may be wildly divergent, with disagreements about teaching style, textbooks, and even the basic principles of social learning. One teacher may want to use drama and role play, while another may reject such strategies. One teacher may want the students to move out into the streets for real experiences in societal issues, while another may see this as trendy and with no real purpose.

In a school where the teachers have different views resulting in divergent rather than emergent strategies, conflict can arise. Central directives and external influences fall on deaf ears. The staff of the school are unreceptive to external strategies because they cannot reach agreement amongst themselves about what constitutes 'good' or 'bad' strategy.

The link is in the values that anchor the decisions about strategy (see Figure 6.3). For emergent strategy to be cohesive and uniting, rather than divergent and even destructive, the school as an organisation must begin with a single set of core values. Where it has clearly defined what it seeks to achieve, and all employees know this purpose, the strategies which emerge are more likely to be coherent and effective.

Figure 6.3   Values: Strategic Refinement

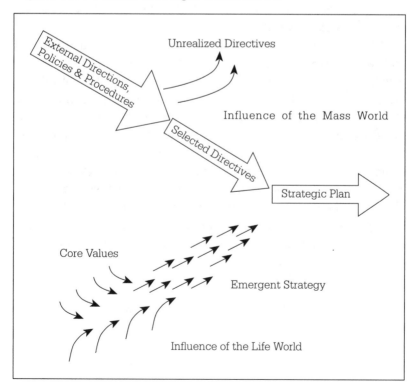

When faced with choices about external strategies, the organisation with a single, clearly determined set of values will be able to make the right decisions about what to accept and what to reject. In other words, it will be a school able to formulate a holistic strategic plan that is a blend of both the internal strategies emerging from the people (the life world) who form the organisation and the external strategies that impinge on the school from outside its boundaries (the mass world).

Summary

We have now laid the basis for a values-based approach to strategic planning, an approach which we see as the most viable one in a world characterised by complex change and uncertainty. We have defined organisational values and the purposes they serve. We have given examples of good value statements and contrasted these with statements which are less than useful. The latter usually represent mere ideals, whereas good statements are developed in such a way that the school can anchor its everyday decisions in them.

We have discussed shifting societal values, espoused values and values-driven change, and have begun to look at the content of value statements. We have also examined the notion of values-driven schools and have provided one conception of the values that might drive future schools. The importance of all organisational stakeholders being involved is paramount if the process is to be effective. Schools have a special role to play in relation to values, because they are involved in teaching values to students. With that in mind, we repeat the warning that if schools fail to identify the key values and beliefs which underpin the thinking of employees and the community, they run the risk of reproducing in their children irrelevant and contextually inappropriate values.

CHAPTER 7

Comparing strategic planning processes

Introduction

When teachers are given a copy of their school's strategic plan – or school improvement plan – and feel threatened by it; when they attack the plan as unworkable, unrealistic or even unreadable; when teachers actively begin to reject the plan and criticise it disloyally, it is not because they intuitively reject change or because, as Kaufman (1992, p. 77) suggests, there is some sort of 'built-in clash between proactive planning and many people's egos' – it is because the process of strategic planning that has been used is inappropriate.

Whatever system your school is in, you have almost certainly been required at some time to produce a plan for the future. Many schools, though, have little experience of such planning. As a result, planning processes more suited to other types of operation are implemented. Such processes may have relevance to motives like wiping out the competition or maximising profit margins, but have little to do with attaining educational objectives. These models of planning are typically top-down approaches. In this chapter, we shall describe the two most common top-down approaches currently being used in schools, and then we shall contrast them with a values-based approach. Our purpose, therefore, is to show the advantages of our approach by demonstrating how it is different from currently prevalent processes.

Traditional Strategic Planning Processes

Schools in many systems have had to learn the language of strategic planning, including terms such as environmental scan and SWOT analysis. In most cases, the techniques are failing to meet the schools' needs. Also imported is the planning model in which strategy is derived from one person's vision. Whether the vision is appropriate or whether there is a need for commitment are issues which are often ignored. The plans may look attractive, but during the first episode of major disruptive change, support usually disintegrates. Plans are then put aside and sometimes forgotten.

Some schools pretend to plan collaboratively by involving stakeholders, but the nature of the involvement may be peripheral and may fail to generate any degree of commitment. These schools 'consult' people, but that is commonly seen as a euphemism for informing them of decisions already made.

If consultation is one widely used way of stemming true involvement, another is the 'planning committee'. This may comprise some senior personnel and representatives of teachers and parents. Representatives, though, provide only samples of beliefs and are rarely able to provoke the dialogue that is necessary amongst all stakeholders if their support is to be won. Involvement, as Semler (1993, p. 76) discovered in Brazil, is about far more than just listening to the 'noise of bees making buzzing sounds in the air'.

The 'deficit' planning model, as we have already described, is based on the principle of analysing the gap between what the school is doing and what it should be doing, and then taking action to close the gap. In schools, this may mean:

- assessing the state of programmes and student achievement;
- identifying priorities of the education system and referring to the vision or mission statement; and
- developing a plan to change timetables, staff deployment, syllabi

and a range of other things with the intention of remedying the deficiency.

A Top-down Approach: Using Planning Consultants

A common process with which most of us are familiar is the top-down planning model, where a plan is developed with a senior management focus. A typical process is shown in Figure 7.1.

The model provides a comprehensive overview of a well-known top-down process of strategic planning. It is the sort of

Figure 7.1   A Traditional Strategic Planning Model

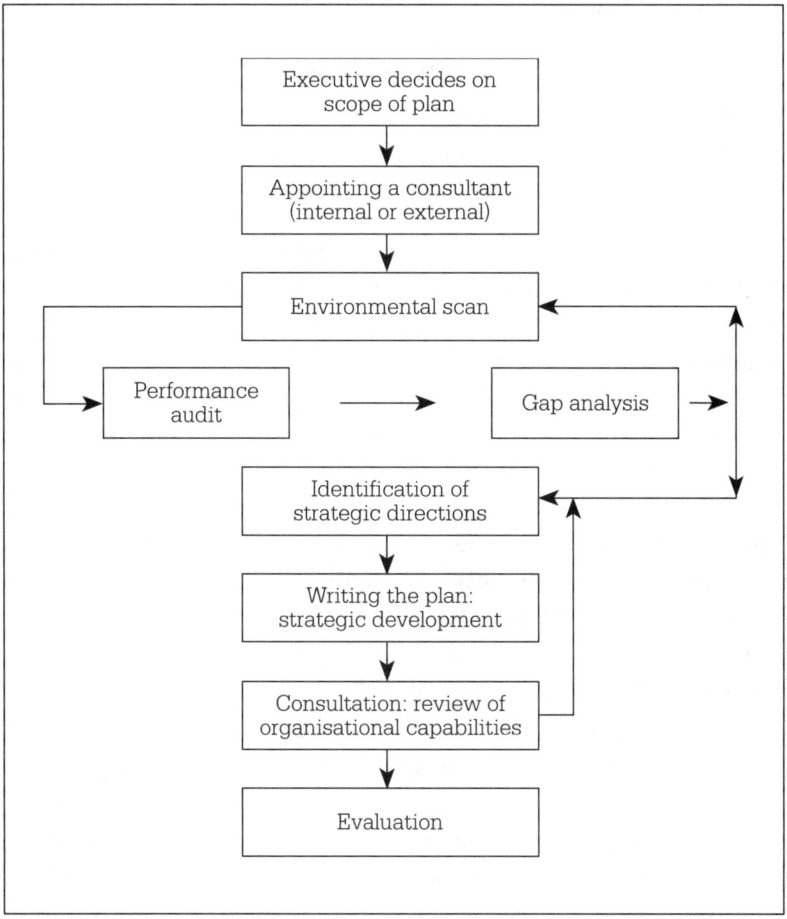

model which is taught in most mainstream management programmes. It has several stages or steps, and we shall take you briefly through these.

Step 1: Executive Decides on Scope of Plan

Top management decides to review current operations and reevaluate organisational direction. A plan of operation is devised which will enable the organisation to meet set goals. The decision to review may be made by the boss or it may be prompted by unacceptable levels of organisational performance.

The plan may be guided by a vision or mission statement, and may set targets and performance indicators. Such targets may be expressed thus:

◆ Effectively increase parental participation in the school.

◆ Review the existing timetable structure.

◆ Redefine senior staff roles and responsibilities.

◆ Review the performance management policy.

The support of an internal or external consultant may be enlisted, and the scope of the plan will be defined. For example, if the plan entails some cost cutting, the plan's scope will determine where those cuts can be made. It may also explain what should not be covered in the review. For example, a principal may state that, while the strategic plan may cover the school's efficiency and effectiveness, it will not look at curriculum or classroom practice.

Setting the aims, purposes and scope of the strategic plan is the job of senior management. Such aims may be consistent with the leader's vision or with corporate mission as defined by a previous management regime.

Step 2: Appointing a Consultant

The plan's author may be a consultant. This person may be someone hired from outside (like a management consultancy firm or a university), or it may be someone internal to the organisation. The advantage of using the former, it is claimed, is that someone can look at the organisation without bias or vested interest. Another claimed advantage is that the consultant can bring in successful ready-made solutions to similar problems that have been faced elsewhere. The advantages of using an internal consultant are ones of cost, commitment to the organisation, that he or she can be trusted by colleagues, and that confidential information can be kept within the school.

Whether the consultant is external or internal, the person is usually selected on the basis of his or her views being in line with those of senior management.

Step 3: Environmental Scan

An environmental scan takes place to discover the deficiencies: what is the school not doing right? what is it not delivering? what is expected of the school that is not happening? what could be done better, more efficiently? and so forth. Such questions may be informed by what other organisations are doing, what the clients want of the school, what the central agency expects and what society demands.

A common scanning tool is a SWOT analysis (Strengths, Weaknesses, Opportunities and Threats). An environmental scan based on the SWOT model may consider factors such as the organisation's competitors, weaknesses in terms of personnel and resources, opportunities for development that have not yet being explored, and the client's view of where the strengths of the organisation lie. In most traditional texts, the SWOT analysis is described as examining the strengths and weaknesses inside the organisation, and the opportunities and threats which lie in wait outside the organisation.

Step 4: Performance Audit

The next task is to look at what the organisation is doing, at its achievements, processes and structures. This involves the consultant in analysis of documentation, observing people and talking to them.

This internal review may sometimes employ quantitative methods of assessing people's work and contribution. For example, it may entail reaching conclusions on whether a particular job deserves a certain level of pay, and all sorts of job evaluation instruments may be used to make an 'objective' decision. Quantitative methods may also be used to measure school culture and climate to determine employees' happiness, morale, and so forth.

The consultant conducting an internal audit may be greeted with either suspicion or enthusiasm. For some, the audit is seen as distrust on the part of senior management; for others, it is an opportunity to voice their deeply held concerns about their unhappiness in the organisation. Whatever the reaction, the audit should provide senior management with an accurate and detailed study of the structures, capabilities, current achievements and resources of the organisation. This includes an in-depth analysis of its potential for development and change. The reason for this analysis is to be able to compare what the organisation is doing with what it should be doing in order to identify the deficit to be rectified in the resulting strategic plan.

Step 5: Gap Analysis

The 'gap' is the difference between the ideal and the actual. The purpose of the analysis is to determine how the school can improve what it is doing to better meet the needs of its clients. For some organisations, closing the gap may entail major changes, including restructuring, reengineering and rethinking. For other organisations, the changes may be minimal.

Gap analysis is a highly subjective and micropolitical process that involves senior management in evaluating what the 'true' nature of the deficit is and how it can be addressed. It is subjective because it is informed by personal interpretation and the individual's experiences and social understanding. It is micropolitical because the analysis is based on a process of argumentation that is affected by the degree of influence which the individuals involved are able to bring to bear.

Currently, most gap analysis in education is driven by economic rationalist thinking. Thus, typical solutions include restructuring, 'smarter' work practices, 'trimming the fat', getting 'back to basics' and cost cutting. It is not surprising that teachers face reviews with as much enthusiasm as a visit to the dentist.

At the school level, most gap analysis falls within the principal's domain. Interpreting what the school needs to do is the responsibility of the transformational leader, the one who has leadership vision. Such leaders need to be able to transform people: change their minds and hearts, their visions, insights and understandings; clarify purposes; make behaviour congruent with beliefs, principles or values; and bring about changes that are permanent, self-perpetuating and momentum building (Covey, 1992).

Step 6: Identification of Strategic Directions

With the gap analysis complete, senior management now prioritises those areas of major focus for organisational change. This results in a series of strategic options or business solutions called 'strategic directions'. These are determined by senior management and are influenced by economic and political considerations.

Step 7: Writing the Plan: Strategic Development

The next stage is to plan the implementation of the changes. The plan would normally contain the following:

◆ Vision – A statement that describes the desired future of the organisation. This is usually written by the principal.

◆ Mission – A statement of school purpose. This is often mixed up with the vision statement.

◆ Values – In traditional strategic planning, values are no more than philosophies or guiding ideals for how the staff of an organisation should conduct themselves, and how the organisation as a whole will behave towards its clients. Terms like integrity, honesty and quality are frequently used.

◆ Key result areas – These are more usually known as goals or targets.

◆ Performance indicators – Also known as outcomes or objectives, these are seen to be measurable (quantifiable) and testable signs that the plan is in operation and that change has occurred. They are given as actual achievements that would mark the attainment of the plan. Performance indicators would be written for all goals or targets. Performance indicators are usually written with 'benchmarks' that describe standards, time lines and accountability.

◆ Strategies – Also described as operational plans, these are the activities that are put into place in order to achieve the key result areas and performance indicators.

Step 8: Consultation: Review of Organisational Capabilities

The strategic planning document is then released for broad consultation. During the consultative process, organisational units are charged with reviewing the proposed plan and with formulating implementation or action plans. Put simply, they have to put the plan into action. This is the point where employees may become disengaged because they dispute what is possible and what is not.

Step 9: Evaluation

The final stage in the top-down strategic planning process involves an evaluation. After a given period of time, certain questions are asked, like, has the organisation achieved its target changes? has the organisation achieved set performance indicators? has the strategic plan itself achieved what the leaders or senior management set as objectives at the beginning of the process? and has the organisation changed in ways that better meet its own and clients' needs?

A Committees Approach

A variation of the traditional top-down approach to strategic planning involves the use of committees. It is often described as a collaborative approach. The following statement by a high school principal illustrates the main tenets of the method:

■ 'We are very enlightened in this school. All our strategic planning is based on the input of our staff. We have formed a committee to develop the plan, and invited each member of staff to join one of the various committees that are dealing with various aspects of the plan. We have a committee investigating all the important areas of the school: for example, the Curriculum Committee, the Behavioural Management Committee, Gifted Children's Programme, and the Sports and Athletics Committee. Each committee is responsible for writing an action plan that addresses the problems within their charter, and presenting this to the executive for ratification and adoption within the overall school plan. A member of the school's executive is on each committee'. ■

While the principal may see it as a collaborative approach, in reality, members of committees may not truly represent the views of others. Consequently, plans developed in this way are still highly problematic.

The committee-based process is founded on the same principles and stages as the top-down consultancy model, but the committee, and not a consultant, is now responsible for the plan. Figure 7.2 illustrates the process.

Figure 7.2   The Committee-based Strategic Planning Model

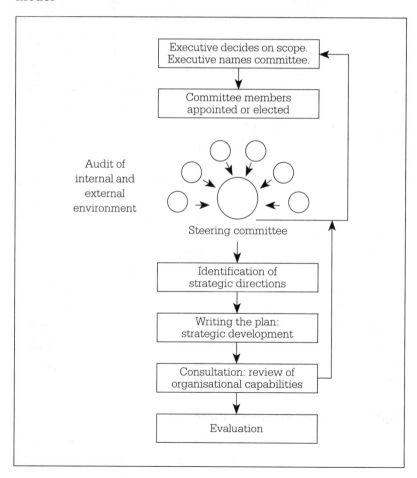

Executive Decides on Purpose and Scope of Strategic Plan. Executive also Appoints Staff to Planning Committee

Strategic planning begins with the decision by senior management that it is necessary to review current operations, decide on future directions and develop a plan of operation that will enable the organisation to achieve set goals. The purpose of the review is laid out along with the plan's scope.

A number of committees are formed. The first is a management or strategic plan committee. This committee then forms sub-committees to cover the various areas of concern. These may include a curriculum committee, a professional development committee, a behavioural management committee, and so on.

The membership of the various committees is usually decided by senior management to ensure they are functionally, and in some cases politically, sound. This involves placing members on each committee who are known to support the dominant values of the organisation. It is the role of committees to undertake scans, audits and analyses in their areas of responsibility. The professional development sub-committee, for example, would have the responsibility of surveying the professional development needs of staff. It would be responsible for identifying the deficit between what the school should be doing and what it is currently doing in its professional development provision. The sub-committee would also look at resources and at what other schools are doing. A report would be presented to the main strategic planning committee, which would pull together all the reports from the various sub-committees.

In some schools, sub-committees have been set up for everything imaginable and teachers have had to be involved whether they liked it or not. The problem with so many committees is that people spend an inordinate amount of time in meetings, and the process of information gathering usually means that surveys and questionnaires abound. This is ineffective participation, which leads eventually to frustration and confusion.

Identification of Strategic Directions

Once committee reports are completed they are submitted to the management committee for ratification. Individual reports are synthesised to form the strategic analysis from which senior management can prioritise areas of major focus for long-term organisational activity.

Committees tend to produce long lists of recommendations which naturally reflect their interests, but economic and political dictates prevent most of them being accepted. Thus senior management retains strict control over the planning process.

While the committee approach is based on notional participation, it also stimulates inter-group rivalry as committees vie for scarce resources. The more influential committees are, the more they are able to determine strategic direction.

It can be seen how easily frustration can occur if much hard work and well-argued recommendations fail to find senior management support. The aggrieved frequently observe that decisions are taken even before the formation of committees.

Writing the Plan: Strategic Development

With priorities determined, a plan is now developed to implement the required changes. It may be stated in the introduction that the plan is the result of extensive collaboration, but, to teachers and possibly parents, it is seldom recognizable as their work. In some cases, their efforts have been ignored to the extent that there is bitterness and resentment.

Consultation: Review of Organisational Capabilities

The plan is then distributed to organisational units, which are charged with developing implementation or action plans. Disagreements may arise, since constraints have not been thought through or changes may not be seen as necessary.

Evaluation

While the committees have been disbanded by now, the management committee is retained as a review body to evaluate the progress of the plan's implementation.

Committee processes rarely result in plans that are widely accepted or practically useful. Those involved may become committed to certain ideas which they formulate in their groups, but these ideas are seldom accepted or implemented. The process also provides a platform for those who are politically influential, and with competing interest groups attempting to advance their own positions, the planning process may lead to frustration and anger.

The Values Based Strategic Planning Process

We now turn our attention to a brief examination of the values based strategic planning process. A full step-by-step explanation of this approach is provided in Section 2.

Values based strategic planning is unlike traditional strategic planning in that it is not based on the principles of gap analysis and then planning how to rectify the deficit. Rather, it is a positive process which focuses first on people and on enabling them to attain what they believe is the organisation's purpose.

Garmston and Wellman (1995, p. 8) suggest that organisations today must continually ask two vital questions: 'Who are we?' and 'What is our purpose?' They propose that schools should be adaptive and should work in this direction by:

♦ basing decisions on the two questions posed above and filtering responses through agreed core values;

♦ shifting decision-making authority to the people most influenced by the decision;

♦ restructuring the day and year to increase the time teachers have to interact collegially with one another;

♦ setting outcomes and standards that signal a passion for excellence and attention to qualities that are based on real-world needs; and

♦ supporting staff members in collaboratively setting and working towards self-defined goals.

Developing a culture in which those principles might feature is an important consideration. The culture should be one of learning, where learning is characterised by risk taking, ideas, a commitment to change and innovation, and a belief in what is happening. People should know that what they value is shared by the school's senior management. Schools of the future, we argue, should develop cultures which are based on *putting values into action*.

Strategic planning is a process that allows people to *position* themselves to take the best advantage of their skills, competencies and beliefs. 'The person who knows the most about doing the job, and who should make decisions about the job, is the person doing it' (Carr and Littman, 1990, p. 11). Thus, employees must have ownership of the strategic plan. It must be something that happens 'inside' the school, while being informed about what is happening 'outside'. The plan charts how the organisation might influence its future, not by filling gaps, but by enabling people to realise what they value.

Following is a brief overview of the stages of the values based strategic planning process. The practical details of the model will be explained in the next chapter.

Step 1: Introduction
Step 2: Values Scan

The values scan involves all staff and interested community members (including parents). Participants map out what the school stands for and what it should achieve.

Step 3: Critical Issues

Participants think through the critical issues which are likely to have the most impact on the school's intentions. They provide knowledge about key issues, system mandates, central directions, community politics and possible policy changes.

Step 4: Writing a Mission Statement

Participants now develop a statement of intent (mission) from the collated values of the organisation. The mission defines the purpose of the strategic plan.

Step 5: Keep, Change and Try

The key result areas of the strategic plan are delineated through a process called 'keep, change and try'.

Keep: What is the school doing that is worth keeping?

Change: What changes should be made to current practices?

Try: What innovations, initiatives or ideas should be tried out?

Step 6: Collating and Prioritising Key Result Areas

The results of the 'keep, change and try' exercise are collated and prioritised. These priorities become the 'key result areas'.

Step 7: Focus Sheets

The main key result areas (about eight to ten) are used as a basis for developing 'focus sheets'. These explain how the key result areas will be achieved. Focus sheets include key result areas, strategies, performance indicators, key tasks and resources.

Step 8: Pulling It Together

The completed focus sheets are assembled into what is the first draft of the strategic plan. The participants decide on the focus sheets' order of priority, that is, the order in which the key result areas should be tackled. A review date is set.

Step 9: Client Scan (Optional)

If parents or other community members have not yet been involved in the development of the plan, a client scan should be undertaken to seek their input before finalising the strategic plan.

In the final part of this chapter, we contrast the top-down approaches we have described with the values-based approach to planning.

Differences between Planning Approaches

Table 7.1 presents a summary and comparison of the major stages in three different strategic planning processes: the traditional top-down consultancy-type method, the committee approach, and the approach which starts from the basis of organisational stakeholders' values.

Table 7.1   A Comparison of Three Strategic Planning Models

Top-down strategic planning	Committee-based strategic planning	Values based strategic planning
Scope and purpose Begins with the school's senior management identifying the scope and purpose of the strategic plan.	**Scope and purpose** Begins with the school's senior management identifying the scope and purpose of the strategic plan.	**Values scan** Begins with a values scan involving staff and community. Scope and purpose of plan distilled from concerns raised by participants.
Responsibility An internal or external consultant is engaged and given approximately three to six months to develop the plan.	**Responsibility** A management committee is formed to oversee the strategic plan. Staff nominated to join sub-committees to examine aspects of the school's operation. The process usually takes several months.	**Responsibility** Development of plan is seen as responsibility of whole staff and interested community members. The plan is drawn up as part of a day's workshop or at a series of meetings over a short time period.
Identifying goals Consultant identifies what the school should be doing and achieving by referring to the community and policy directives, and to national and international influences.	**Identifying goals** Sub-committees review aspects of the organisation's past and current operation. Recommendations are made along with goals for their areas of concern.	**Identifying goals** All participants identify the key result areas.
Current performance An audit of the school is undertaken by consultant. Audit is to determine what the school is currently doing and achieving. It may involve review of work practices.	**Negotiation** Sub-committees negotiate or compete for greater share of limited resources. Groups argue for their focus areas being given greater priority than others.	**Critical issues** Participants identify external factors that may impact on the school's plans.

Table 7.1 (*continued*)

Top-down strategic planning	Committee-based strategic planning	Values based strategic planning
Strategic direction Based on audit reports and environmental scans, the strategic direction is determined by the organisation's executive. This usually takes the form of guiding principles or future strategies.	**Strategic direction** Reports of committees collated by management committee, followed by the development of a single plan for the school. Senior management determines strategic direction.	**Strategic direction** All participants are involved in a consensual process of setting priorities for action.
Action plans All the school's work units are required to submit detailed plans on how they will achieve the strategic directions. These include action plans, performance indicators and resource reviews.	**Action plans** All the school's work units are required to submit detailed plans on how they will achieve the strategic directions. These include action plans, performance indicators and resource reviews.	**Implementation** Participants are involved in converting the key result areas into action through a 'focus sheet' process.
Final strategic plan Based on the action plans submitted, the executive makes decisions on restructuring, and a final plan is produced and distributed. The plan is fixed.	**Final strategic plan** Based on the action plans submitted, the executive makes decisions on restructuring, and a final plan is produced and distributed. The plan is fixed.	**Contingency planning** A strategic plan is printed. The plan has removable focus sheets that can be replaced as key result areas are either achieved or changed. The plan is flexible.
Evaluation Strategic plan is evaluated in preparation for a new planning cycle.	**Evaluation** Strategic plan is evaluated in preparation for a new planning cycle.	**Review** A review date is set when the key result areas are evaluated.

It is clear from the summary table that there are many advantages of a values-based approach beyond those of involvement of the people who are most affected by change. Strategic planning, in most traditional approaches, has become unwieldy, unrealistic and time consuming. In the values-based approach, much of the process can be completed in one day, and although there are several unfamiliar terms and procedures, they are neither unmanageable nor difficult. The whole process is simple to operate. And it works! The evidence to date suggests that values based strategic planning generates genuine commitment amongst those who participate, and it ensures that the school addresses the strategic issues which need to be high on the agenda. By achieving this, the school is able to exert some considerable influence on its future and on the way in which it interacts with its environment. That is hardly the case with traditional approaches. There is little to suggest either that commitment is evident amongst organisational members as a result of the planning process or that intended outcomes are actually achieved. Indeed, there are clear indications that, in many cases, the planning process remains just that: a planning process, with the resulting documents being filed away, soon to be forgotten so that normal service may resume as soon as possible.

We hope that we have made a persuasive case for an organisational approach which both values its people and which draws on its people's values as a fundamental process of encountering change. In the next section, we give detailed guidance on how the approach works and the steps you might take to implement it effectively in your institution.

Values Based Strategic Planning: A Practical Guide

CHAPTER 8

Values based strategic planning

Introduction

This section of the book is designed as a practical handbook which will enable you to take your school effectively through the process of strategic planning. It provides a step-by-step guide to a collaborative process which has been used with considerable success in many organisations. These include primary and secondary schools, university faculties, vocational education colleges, Department of Education offices, civil defence units, police organisations and several small business units.

Our focus here is on schools, and the approach has indeed been used with considerable success in educational institutions in several countries. We have proved it works. Using this process, you will be able to involve the whole staff and community of your organisation in a sequence of activities that results in the writing of a meaningful and relevant strategic plan. It will be meaningful for the following reasons:

- It will be a plan that has been written by the whole school community and not just by a representative committee or the organisation's administration.
- It will be written in a short period of time, causing little interruption to normal activities.
- It will generate a feeling of ownership amongst your employees

and community members, since they will have been involved rather than merely consulted.

♦ It will convince those involved that it is a real exercise which leads to tangible results.

♦ It will show clearly people's respective roles in putting the strategic plan into action.

♦ It will serve as a basis for evaluation of the school's programmes.

♦ The process of planning will itself be a valuable exercise, as it enables people to debate critical issues, agendas for action and priority preferences in a stimulating way, and it leads to enormous gains in understanding amongst organisational members.

How Is Planning Carried Out?

We shall now take you through a series of steps which will lead to the development of a strategic plan. These steps, which include various activities and exercises, can be completed in just one day. If it is not possible to devote an entire day's workshop to the process, you will need to arrange separate sessions for the stages. With that in mind, we have provided a time allocation for each of the steps so that you will know how much time to arrange for each session.

The process is designed to involve all members of the school's staff and as many parents as possible. You may wish to involve also other members of your school's community. Everyone should be seated in the same room.

It may not be possible for you to involve people from outside the school in the planning process. In such circumstances, it is possible to do the planning effectively, but you would have to undertake a survey of your clients, and for that purpose, we have provided the optional step 9.

Here is a breakdown of the full day's planning session (breaks would be inserted at suitable times):

Step 1	Introduction	30 minutes
Step 2	Values Scan	60 minutes
Step 3	Critical Issues	20 minutes
Step 4	Writing a Mission Statement	20 minutes

Step 5	Keep, Change and Try	
	Keep	20 minutes
	Change	20 minutes
	Try	30 minutes
Step 6	Collating and Prioritising Key Result Areas	30 minutes
Step 7	Focus Sheets	120 minutes
Step 8	Pulling It Together, Setting a Review Date	30 minutes
Step 9	Client Scan (Optional)	As required

Each of these steps is described in detail using the following headings:

At a Glance

Provides a brief overview of the step and, where appropriate, suggests the time which may be involved.

Purpose

Explains the main purpose of the step.

Objectives

Describes the objectives and intended outcomes of the step.

Making This Step Successful

Identifies factors which are critical to the success of the step. This category may also include 'hints' on what to highlight during the step or the questions which may arise. Some mini-workshops or activities may be included.

Directions

Gives details about what you should do or say as a facilitator during the step.

Useful Advice

In this section we share ideas, problems and variations to the scheme that we have encountered when running the values-based approach in various organisations.

Worksheets

If appropriate, we give you sample worksheets, ideas for overhead transparencies (OHTs) or sample activities to use in the step.

A Summary of the Steps in the Values-based Process

Values based strategic planning is a continuous process, but for ease of explanation, we have broken the process down into discrete steps. We now explain in summary form what happens in each of the steps and suggest a time frame.

Step 1 ■ Introduction

Time: 30 minutes

The values based strategic planning process is explained briefly. The session begins with welcome remarks, and it is stressed that the approach is genuinely collaborative. The facilitator then provides an outline of the day's activities, followed by a description of what the strategic plan will look like and of the benefits to the school.

Step 2 ■ Values Scan

Time: 60 minutes

Step 2 has three phases:

Phase A	Individuals write five value statements.
Phase B	Small groups of three to six people collaborate to produce one set of value statements from their individual ideas.
Phase C	Representatives of each of the groups come together to use their group values to produce a single set of value statements for the school.

Step 3 ■ Critical Issues

Time: 20 minutes

The critical issues that might impact on the school and affect its plans are mapped out. Participants are encouraged to reveal all that they know about the key issues, system mandates, central departmental directions, community politics, policy changes, or any other impacting factor that might affect the organisation in the near future.

Break

Time: Approximately 20 minutes

It is good to plan a time when people can interact and discuss what has happened so far. It also provides time to do some photocopying or word processing of value statements in preparation for subsequent steps.

Step 4 ■ Writing a Mission Statement

Time: 20 minutes

A mission statement is developed from the final list of value statements. Groups work to devise a mission statement, and then their attempts are submitted to the scrutiny of all other groups, with one statement finally selected.

Step 5 ■ Keep, Change and Try

Step 5 has three phases:

Phase A   Keep: What should the school continue to do?

Phase B   Change: What changes should be made?

Phase C   Try: What innovations, initiatives or ideas would staff and community members like to try out in the future?

We now look at these three phases in more detail.

Keep

Time: 20 minutes

What do participants believe the organisation should carry on doing? They are asked to identify the programmes, activities, policies or structures that the school currently has that they feel should be retained.

Change

Time: 20 minutes

What do participants believe should be done differently? What should the school change over the next six to thirty-six months? Participants are asked to identify the changes they feel need to be made to the programmes, activities, policies or structures of the school in order to make the institution more relevant, effective or efficient.

Try

Time: 30 minutes

Given the opportunity, what innovations, ideas or initiatives are worth trying to see if they would improve the school's ability to achieve its mission and values? Participants are urged to come up with ideas that the school might try out with a view to making improvement gains.

Step 6 ■ Collating and Prioritising Key Result Areas

Time: 30 minutes

The results of the 'keep, change and try' exercise are collated and prioritised. These ideas are then known as the 'key result areas'.

Step 7 ■ Focus Sheets

Time: 120 minutes

The top eight to ten key result areas are used as the basis for developing 'focus sheets'. These describe how the critical success factors will be achieved by the school and will include key result areas, strategies, performance indicators, key tasks and resources. These focus sheets are the main operational elements of the strategic plan.

Step 8 ■ Pulling It Together

Time: 30 minutes

The completed focus sheets are pulled together into what is the first draft of the strategic plan. Participants decide what the priorities should be, the order in which the key result areas should be attempted. A review date is then set.

Step 9 ■ Client Scan (Optional)

If community members (clients) are not involved in the process as direct participants, it is recommended that the process involves a strategy of client scanning or surveying.

The process of scanning we recommend avoids paperwork, but instead relies on making contact – usually by telephone – with members of the community to let them know that their input is valued.

An overview has been provided of what each stage entails. The next part of this chapter goes into the finer points of detail of the process steps.

Introduction

Session time: 30 minutes

Step 1 ■ Introduction

Step 2 ■ Values Scan

Step 3 ■ Critical Issues

Step 4 ■ Mission Statement

Step 5 ■ Keep, Change and Try

Step 6 ■ Key Result Areas

Step 7 ■ Focus Sheets

Step 8 ■ Pulling It Together

Step 9 ■ Client Scan (Optional)

At a Glance

The purpose of Step 1 is to begin the process. The schedule for the day is set, targets are established, and the key principles of values based strategic planning are outlined.

Participants will know already that the purpose of the day is to formulate a strategic plan and that their involvement is real and vital. They may have been asked to think about some goals that they would like set, so they will probably arrive at the meeting with at least some ideas about what is important to them.

All teachers are expected to take part. Parents and community members should also be invited to participate, as well as auxiliary staff, including administrative support personnel.

The process begins with a 10-minute welcome by either the principal or the chair of the school's council or board.

At this point, the facilitator for the day (this may be a member of the teaching staff or management team, or a consultant) describes what the day's outcome will be: a strategic plan. All participants should have a clear picture of what the strategic plan will contain, so the facilitator should use a transparency to show the details.

This is also a time for informing people about what the strategic plan is to be used for, and for reinforcing the fact that their involvement is real: their deliberations and decisions will indeed combine to form a plan that will be used.

Purpose

This step is to show participants the shape the strategic plan will take and to convince them that their involvement matters. While the process itself is of prime importance, it is useful to explain to participants what the printed document will look like.

Objectives

By the end of Step 1, participants will:

- ◆ know that a printed strategic plan will be produced and the shape it will take; and
- ◆ understand the nature of their involvement in helping to make the school's future successful.

Making This Step Successful

The following points should be kept in mind:

- ◆ Everyone must be involved: teaching staff, support staff, parents and other members of the community with an interest in the school.
- ◆ The process works well with large groups. Try to mix parents and staff together at tables.
- ◆ Lead from the top, develop from the bottom. The principal must demonstrate clearly his or her commitment to the process, and give guarantees that, wherever possible, the outcomes of the process will be supported.

◆ Where the school is answerable to a central authority, staff must have assurances that the authority is supportive of the process and will not hinder their involvement.

◆ The executive staff, including the principal, should be a part of the planning process on an equal footing with others. They should take part in all the activities, and that is why it is useful to have an external facilitator.

Directions

The facilitator should explain the process, including the time schedule, and should outline the contents of the strategic plan. Here is a summary of what should be covered by the facilitator in the introduction:

General Remarks

The following remarks, expressed in the facilitator's own words, set the scene:

> Our future, our success and our existence as a school is anchored by what we believe we are here to achieve.
>
> The people who know best about what we should aim to achieve and how we should improve our school are teachers, school employees, parents and all those with a genuine interest in the school. We need your involvement in this process.
>
> Strategic planning is a process that is ongoing. What we are doing here today will help us to learn much about ourselves and our school, and that in turn will help the school to improve.

Explaining the Strategic Plan

Using a transparency, the facilitator should describe what will be in the strategic plan document that is produced at the end of the process. It will contain:

◆ Foreword
◆ Introduction
◆ Who we are
◆ Value statements and mission statement
◆ Critical issues

- Key result areas (keep, change, try)
- Focus sheets: Key result areas, strategies, performance indicators, key tasks, resources
- Optional: Client scan, financial plan

We shall now explain what is included in each section of the strategic plan.

Foreword: A brief paragraph written by the chair of the school's council or another individual of significance to the school. The foreword should invite the reader to be a part of the school and congratulate the staff and community members who were involved in producing this plan.

Introduction: A brief statement from the principal. The introduction should explain how the strategic plan was produced, with particular emphasis on the collaborative input of staff and community members.

Who we are: A brief one-page description of the school, its demographics, its location and history.

Value statements and mission statement: The four to seven value statements that summarise what the staff and community members believe the school exists to achieve. The mission statement describes the purpose of the school.

Critical issues: A list of the known and predicted factors that are outside the school's control and which might impact on the school over the next year or so.

Key result areas: Known as 'keep, change and try', the key result areas are those activities, programmes, objectives, policies, structures and ways of doing things that the participants have identified as crucial for the school to meet its stated intent and for it to meet the needs of its community.

Focus sheets: The focus sheets comprise the bulk of the strategic plan. They are essentially individual summary sheets, one for each critical success factor, that provide the performance indicators, strategies, key tasks and resource implications. These focus sheets provide the details of what the school intends to do in the coming year or two. They make the strategic plan practical and realistic. The number of focus sheets will vary depending on the size and scope of the plan. The sheets are not permanent, but should be replaced or removed as each critical success factor is achieved (or becomes redundant).

Client scan (optional): This is entirely optional and found only in those strategic plans where the community (clients) has not been involved in the planning process.

Financial plan (optional): This is entirely optional and found only in those plans where financial planning is integral to strategy and is a requirement.

Useful Advice

The session should move along quickly and the facilitator should avoid answering questions about the finer points of detail of the strategic plan, since the participants will find that most of their questions are addressed as the day progresses. So that the facilitator is prepared, here are some typical questions that might be asked:

- What will we gain from the process?
- What assurances do we have that if we do all this work, anything will come of it? (Can we trust you?)
- How much time is involved?
- Why is this any different from the last strategic plan that we had?
- Does this mean more changes? (Should I feel threatened by this? Will it lead to restructuring that may cost me my job or comfortable existence?)

The only difficulties we have encountered in persuading employees of the worth of the process is in those organisations where strategic planning has been imposed in the past and where employees are consequently cynical and suspicious. Some have been vocal in their disbelief that planning is proceeding on a 'bottom-up' basis: 'Are you trying to tell us that the school will listen to what *we* have to say'?

It is not necessary to win over every member of staff at the start. Healthy debate will open up the issues about planning in this way and will do good. The proof of the pudding is in the eating, of course, and once people see that their role is genuine, they will be more than supportive. Those who choose to remain on the periphery will soon learn that they will have little influence on their future by not becoming fully involved.

Worksheet 8.1

The Strategic Plan

◆ Foreword

◆ Introduction

◆ Who we are

◆ Value statements and mission statement

◆ Critical issues

◆ Key result areas (keep, change, try)

◆ Focus sheets: Key result areas; strategies, performance indicators, key tasks, resources

◆ Optional: Client scan, financial plan

Worksheet 8.2

Schedule for the Day

Values based strategic planning

Step 1	Introduction	30 minutes
Step 2	Values Scan	60 minutes
Step 3	Critical Issues	20 minutes
Step 4	Writing a Mission Statement	20 minutes
Step 5	Keep, Change and Try	
	Keep	20 minutes
	Change	20 minutes
	Try	30 minutes
Step 6	Collating and Prioritising Key Result Areas	30 minutes
Step 7	Focus Sheets	120 minutes
Step 8	Pulling It Together, Setting a Review Date	30 minutes

Values scan

Session time: 60 minutes
Step 1 ■ Introduction
Step 2 ■ Values Scan
Step 3 ■ Critical Issues
Step 4 ■ Mission Statement
Step 5 ■ Keep, Change and Try
Step 6 ■ Key Result Areas
Step 7 ■ Focus Sheets
Step 8 ■ Pulling It Together
Step 9 ■ Client Scan (Optional)

Step 2 involves participants in collaboratively deciding on the purpose of the school. A strategic plan needs to be relevant and effective. It cannot be either unless people understand the school's purpose, its *raison d'être*.

This step has three phases:

In the first phase, the participants are each asked to take five pieces of index-size blank paper. They are instructed to write one sentence or statement on each. The five statements must describe their values. A value statement is described as: 'What I believe the organisation exists to achieve'. Participants are instructed to do this by themselves without consultation or discussion. This should take 10 minutes.

In the second phase, the participants are asked to work in small groups of about three to five people to collate their individual statements. This is a process of refining and incorporation to develop a single set of value statements for the group. The time allocated for this is 20 minutes.

Finally, in the third phase, each of the groups selects a representative whose job is to present the group's findings in the final stage of reconciling and incorporating ideas. This leads to one set of value statements for the whole school. This takes 20 minutes.

For the purposes of clarity, this step is described as three phases:

Phase A   Writing individual value statements

Phase B   Collating value statements

Phase C   Producing a single set of corporate value statements

Writing Value Statements

At a Glance

Participants have a short period of time to arrive at five statements which best express their values: what they think the organisation should be seeking to achieve. These values express what is important to the author.

Purpose

This step is vital to the whole process. It has the twin purposes of (a) telling and selling, and (b) establishing the values that anchor decision making in the organisation.

Telling and Selling

As telling and selling is the first activity in the process, it holds the key to fulfilling the participants' expectations of what is to follow. It is 'make or break' time!

Because participants are involved right from the start in expressing their values, the belief is confirmed immediately that the people who know best how to improve the work of the school are those who work and have a real interest in it.

Establishing Values

As you will recall from the earlier part of this book, the key to decision making is an understanding of the values that anchor decisions. The first activity, therefore, is identifying what the values are. To do this, we have to find out what participants' beliefs are about the school's purpose.

Objectives

By the end of this stage, the participants will:

- ◆ have thought about and then written down on five pieces of paper their workplace values; and
- ◆ have had reinforced the necessity of their involvement in the strategic planning process.

Making This Step Successful

To ensure this phase works well, allow 10–15 minutes for participants to write five value statements, each on a separate piece of identical paper. Participants should be instructed not to discuss this task with anyone but to write their own personal work values. Here are some guidelines:

- ◆ Provide some samples of what work-related values might be.
- ◆ Participants must be told that one-word or short-phrase responses are not sufficient. For example, 'I believe in excellence' or 'I believe in equal opportunity' are philosophies or ideals; they are not acceptable as value statements.
- ◆ Participants should be told that their values must be testable; that is, each value must be capable of being used to inform day-to-day decisions.
- ◆ If an external facilitator is used, staff must be openly assured that the facilitator's role is simply to oversee the process and not to be involved in advising on the plan.

Directions

- ◆ Use a comfortable room with tables and chairs.
- ◆ Allow staff to sit where they will, but insist on a mix of people in each group. They may want a friend in the group, but they should not sit in departments or units.
- ◆ Cut your index cards to the same size and colour.

Useful Advice

The number of people involved is not important. We have used this activity many times with various numbers and with considerable success. The largest number we have worked with were the 160 staff of a regional education office, and the smallest were the four staff of a small isolated school.

Worksheet 8.3

Samples of Values from an Office

Honesty

Everything we do, every programme we undertake, will be both credible and fully supportable.

Commitment

Our ethos is one of commitment through loyalty to each other and through dedication to task.

Adaptability

Our culture is a learning culture where the ability to respond to change is highly valued.

Service

We strive to provide quality service based on a thorough understanding of and empathy with the needs of our clients.

Accuracy

Accuracy (whether expressed as attention to detail or correctness of advice) underpins our service to clients.

Teamwork

Our belief in each other as members of a team builds mutual respect and provides for supporting each other in times of need.

Performance

We value an approach which is positive in serving the present needs of our clients and in anticipating and planning for their future needs.

Samples of Values from a School

Staff's professional knowledge should be respected and valued, and staff should be supported to share and gain access to knowledge.

Opportunities should be provided for students, parents and school staff to participate in planning and decision making.

Behavioural management is the responsibility of the whole school community and aims to develop an environment which encourages behaviour which is caring, supportive and co-operative.

Students should respect themselves, others and their environment.

Children learn best when school and parents work in a partnership to provide a supportive learning environment.

Equal access to educational opportunities should be available to all.

Our community should have a collaborative school that is a living place which will grow and change with the community it serves, while providing a quality education for all in a climate of trust, understanding and participation.

Collating Value Statements
At a Glance

Once participants have written their individual values on index cards, the next stage should begin immediately (during the same session). In this stage, the participants are asked to form small groups of about three to five people. The group takes its combined values (fifteen value cards in a group of three) and, through a process of combining ideas and valuing one another's input, produces a single set of five value statements which reflects the group's beliefs about work. This process should take 20 minutes.

Purpose

The main purpose of this phase is to distil values into representative ones across the school. The process itself is of great benefit as people are involved in critical discourse and in listening to others' views. It also provokes a greater level of cross-departmental understanding as Maths teachers listen to English teachers, principals listen to secretaries, teachers listen to parents, and so on.

Objectives

By the end of this stage the participants will:

♦   have worked in groups to distil the individual values down to sets of value statements that are inclusive of the views of many people; and

◆ have worked consensually with their colleagues on issues of belief.

Making This Step Successful

In order for this phase of Step 2 to work effectively, the facilitator should bear the following points in mind:

◆ Inclusiveness – The process of producing a single set of value statements is not based on discarding minority views but on combining similar ideas to create values that encompass the beliefs of all.

◆ Involvement – There is a problem if some people stay on the periphery of the debate and decline involvement.

◆ Time – The activity should be 'snappy', so that participants do not feel time is dragging. Keep the momentum going. If people have not finished, it does not matter: move on. Discourage participants from taking a perfectionist stance, where every word has to be carefully thought out and every sentence refined.

◆ Representativeness – The final list of value statements is representative of commonly agreed values and is not an exhaustive list of opinion.

Directions

At the conclusion of the first phase, when participants have written individual value statements, ask them to move into groups of three (a maximum of five with larger groups).

One of the group members lays his or her value cards down in a row on the table. The other group members read and discuss, and then in turn lay their value cards on top of those on the table, trying to keep similar ideas in the same piles. Through this process the group should end up with five or so piles of cards. The piles of cards thus created will be of value statements of *similar* meaning (it is important to describe the process of laying out the cards in a row in detail and with a demonstration).

When this is finished, each person in the group should have one or two piles of similar value cards. Each person is then responsible for using the information on the cards to write one new value statement on a new, different coloured index card. The resulting value statement should not be a summary of the cards, but a new statement that captures the ideas of the group.

Useful Advice

The key to this process is that participants are being asked to discuss and list their workplace values, not their personal life values, and because they work in the same place, they will commonly hold similar values. They may be worded differently, or there may be a different emphasis applied to some values over others, but the process of distilling the values of the members of the group to a single set of five or six will happen more easily than one might expect.

The best way of thinking about the process is not as one of discarding minority values, but as one of prioritising and confirming what the individuals and groups have known but have never previously put down on paper.

Of course, some individuals may not concur with the commonly accepted values of the workplace. Their views are of critical importance, for they bring a diversity of perspective to the debate, and suppressing their deeply held beliefs – for whatever reason they hold them – will not change their values nor their capacity to influence their decisions and actions. Thus, it is worth exploring divergent values seriously. Do not jump to a quick consensus by marginalising these people because the consensus will be a false one.

Towards One Set of Values
At a Glance

In this third and final phase of Step 2, the participants, who are now in groups, are asked to select one person to represent their group. This representative meets with the representatives of the other groups, and all the representatives are charged with taking their new combined values through the same process of distillation to produce one single set of five value statements that reflect the whole school's beliefs. This should be done in less than 20 minutes.

Purpose

The main purpose of this third phase is to derive a single list of five value statements that are representative of the beliefs of most participants.

The list of values that is finally decided on should not be seen as the only values of the school, but as a list of the dominant values that are broadly identifiable as belonging to the school.

Objectives

By the end of this stage the participants will have developed one set of value statements that are representative of the values underlying the theory of operation of the whole school.

Making This Step Successful

Timing is important. Slow groups should be urged to move on so that the initial impetus is maintained and people do not lose interest.

Directions

At the conclusion of the second phase, when the small groups have written value statements, each group should be asked to select a representative who will carry out the same task on their behalf across all the groups.

One member of the group is told to lay his or her value cards down in a row on the table. The other group members in turn read and discuss, and then lay their value cards on top of those on the table, trying to keep the piles similar in meaning. Through this process the group should end up with five or so piles of cards. The piles of cards thus created will be of value statements of *similar* meaning.

When this is finished, the piles of cards are distributed to group members, each of whom is then responsible for using the information on the cards to write one new value statement on a new, differently coloured index card. The resulting value statement should be a new one which captures the ideas from the pile.

While the group representatives are distilling the final value statements for the whole school, the rest of the participants should be directed to the next step on Critical Issues.

Useful Advice

The first time this process is described, the main questions that arise in the minds of many participants are:

◆ How can the values of fifty or more people be reduced to just five or six statements and be valid?

◆ Does this process not diminish the importance of the individual's values?

As stated earlier, we have used this method with a single group of 160 people. That equates to 700 individual value statements on index cards. In 1 hour we were able to successfully reduce these 700 statements to a final group list of six statements.

Worksheets

While the group is distilling the list of five or six values, the facilitator should display the diagram 'Converting Values to Mission' (shown as a worksheet) on an overhead projector. On completion, the final five or six values are to be written into Worksheet 8.4 for everyone to see.

Worksheet 8.4   Converting Values to Mission

Critical issues

Session time: 20 minutes

Step 1 ■ Introduction
Step 2 ■ Values Scan
Step 3 ■ Critical Issues
Step 4 ■ Mission Statement
Step 5 ■ Keep, Change and Try
Step 6 ■ Key Result Areas
Step 7 ■ Focus Sheets
Step 8 ■ Pulling It Together
Step 9 ■ Client Scan (Optional)

At a Glance

'If only we could have foreseen the change before it hit us, at least we could have been prepared for it'.

Lamenting the imposition of change from factors outside the school's control is often linked to foresight or predictability. Could the change have been predicted? Were there signs that were ignored? Were we blind to what was happening around us?

When developing a strategic plan, the question often arises: how do you allow in your plan for imposed changes or unexpected events? Uncertainty and unpredictability are features of our contemporary organisational world, and sometimes we feel the effects of things that may be happening in distant places and which are seemingly unrelated to education. Whatever type of management or planning the school practises, unexpected change confronts us. It can take the form of a directive from central office, a policy change, staff moving to different jobs, and even economic and political events in other countries.

The values-based approach recognises the inevitability of unexpected and imposed change and builds it into the planning process through an activity called 'critical issues'.

Purpose

The purpose of this step is to make a list of all the major changes that might have an impact on the school in the near future. This is not an exercise in crystal ball gazing, but an attempt to read and interpret some of the signals in the environment. It thus leads to a greater understanding of the school's context. It must be stressed, however, that there is no guarantee that what is identified is either accurate or exhaustive. So why do it? The answer lies in the word understanding. If we understand our context, we are more likely to pick out the issues that matter and that can have an impact on our organisation's future success. There is no certainty. But we raise the odds in our favour.

Objectives

In order to deal with imposed or unpredictable changes, it is important to:

- prepare staff for the fact that they will happen;
- ensure that as far as possible all known imposed changes that are likely to impact on the school are factored into the strategic plan;
- recognise that individual staff members or clients may be able to provide insightful information about future directions or changes that are not apparent to the executive; and
- understand that strategic planning is a flexible, ongoing process, and not a once and for all exercise.

Making This Step Successful

This step works well if participants can indicate when they expect something might happen that could have an impact on the school.

Some examples will often help this process. The facilitator might, for example, provide some known system-mandated changes or government policy changes that will probably affect the school. These might include the date of the introduction of a new Maths curriculum or a new staff performance management procedure. It might be the date when a new building is expected to be completed or a new computer system installed, or when a major staff change is expected.

It is important to emphasise that it is the individual's own knowledge that the group is seeking, since just one person may have valuable insights that have escaped the attention of others.

Directions

Each individual is given a copy of the time continuum worksheet.

Participants are asked to mark on the sheet all the major changes that they think will affect their work. These may be changes which do not have a direct impact on the individual's job but which might have some effect on the school as a whole.

Participants are then formed into small groups based on work unit teams or similar interest teams.

Each group combines the ideas of the individuals and collaboratively develops a full list of the known changes that might affect their work and impact on the school in the future.

Groups reduce individuals' ideas to one list. This is done through a process of rewording issues in order to make them inclusive of larger concerns.

Useful Advice

This process of critical issues identification takes place while a smaller group of participants is working on the final value statements.

The process is energising and even noisy as participants recognise impending changes. Discussions may also dwell on past changes which should have been spotted and which affected morale adversely.

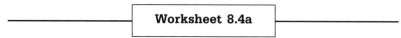

The Critical Issues

Write what you perceive to be the critical issues onto the time scale. You can use the space both above and below the line.

One year ago   NOW   Two years ahead

Celebration Point

The celebration point – which could coincide with a refreshment break – marks the end of a major achievement in the planning process. Participants at this stage have produced a set of value statements which represent organisational purpose. They have also examined their context and identified some of the changes that might have an impact on their school in the near future.

This is a good time to have a break in the process and to celebrate the success of the planning process so far. But while most people are enjoying a well-earned rest, the facilitation team will have to photocopy the value statements and arrange for everyone to receive a copy. This is a clear indication that all contributions are important.

STEP 4

Writing a mission statement

Session time: 20 minutes
Step 1 ■ Introduction
Step 2 ■ Values Scan
Step 3 ■ Critical Issues
Step 4 ■ Mission Statement
Step 5 ■ Keep, Change and Try
Step 6 ■ Key Result Areas
Step 7 ■ Focus Sheets
Step 8 ■ Pulling It Together
Step 9 ■ Client Scan (Optional)

At a Glance

Following a short break, participants are given the printed value statements on a worksheet. Now, the value statements are used to write a mission statement. The participants are divided into small groups of three to six people, and each group is asked to use the value statements as the basis from which to write a mission statement of no more than thirty-two words. This is to be done in 10 minutes. At the end of the allotted time, the mission statements are collected for copying and distribution. For most schools, this can be done almost immediately if there is a copier close by. Participants have 10 minutes in which to read through them and to decide which they, individually, like the most. Each individual participant having made his or her selection, the mission statement which has attracted the most support is adopted for wider circulation and comment.

Purpose

In the values-based approach, the stated intent in the form of a summary mission is derived from organisational values rather than from the executive. Thus, the mission is more likely to be real than fictional and to be congruent with people's beliefs about what the organisation should be doing.

Objectives

By the end of this step, the participants will:

◆ have formed groups and have written a number of possible mission statements based on the agreed value statements of the organisation; and

◆ have identified a worded statement which best expresses what they understand as the school's purpose.

Making This Step Successful

To ensure the success of this session:

◆ everyone must be involved; and

◆ working in small groups, participants should treat the exercise as one of stating the school's mission with creativity and impact. The more innovative it is and the more representative of the school's agreed values, the more likely it is to be adopted.

Directions

During this time, the facilitator should do the following:

Show in sequence on an overhead projector the two worksheets entitled 'Values to Mission' and 'Forming the Mission Statement'. These are shown as worksheets.

Distribute copies of or display the school's value statements.

Describe what a mission statement is and how it should be distilled from the agreed value statements.

Direct participants to form small groups. Each group is required to write a mission statement from the agreed value statements. The mission statements should be thirty-two words or less.

Distribute the completed mission statements and allow individuals to select the one they like the most. The one which wins the most support will become the school's draft mission.

The draft mission statement should be circulated for comment and edited, this to be done over a two-week period.

Useful Advice

At this time it is useful to provide the participants with examples of completed summaries of values with derived mission statements.

People will inevitably ask why there is a thirty-two word limit. The answer is that experience has shown this to be about the most that people can remember comfortably. If the statement is to be a working document which helps to guide decision making, then it should be relatively easy to remember.

Worksheet 8.5 Values into Mission

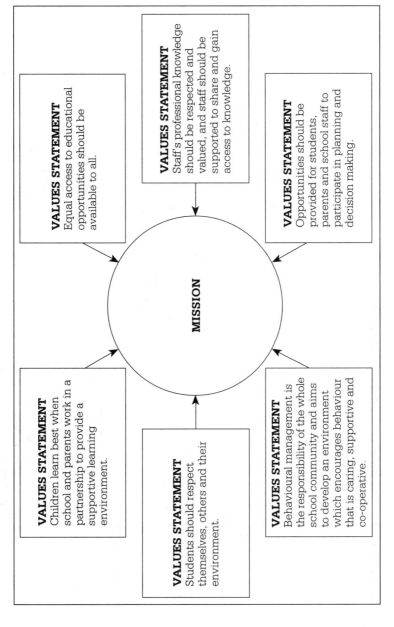

VALUES STATEMENT
Equal access to educational opportunities should be available to all.

VALUES STATEMENT
Staff's professional knowledge should be respected and valued, and staff should be supported to share and gain access to knowledge.

VALUES STATEMENT
Opportunities should be provided for students, parents and school staff to participate in planning and decision making.

VALUES STATEMENT
Children learn best when school and parents work in a partnership to provide a supportive learning environment.

VALUES STATEMENT
Students should respect themselves, others and their environment.

VALUES STATEMENT
Behavioural management is the responsibility of the whole school community and aims to develop an environment which encourages behaviour that is caring, supportive and co-operative.

MISSION

Worksheet 8.6   Sample of Completed Mission

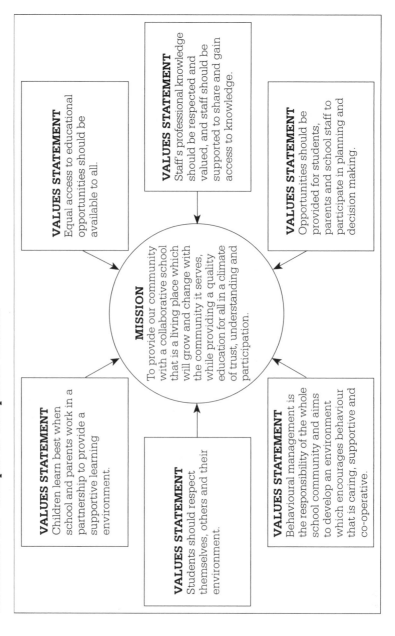

VALUES STATEMENT
Equal access to educational opportunities should be available to all.

VALUES STATEMENT
Staff's professional knowledge should be respected and valued, and staff should be supported to share and gain access to knowledge.

VALUES STATEMENT
Opportunities should be provided for students, parents and school staff to participate in planning and decision making.

MISSION
To provide our community with a collaborative school that is a living place which will grow and change with the community it serves, while providing a quality education for all in a climate of trust, understanding and participation.

VALUES STATEMENT
Children learn best when school and parents work in a partnership to provide a supportive learning environment.

VALUES STATEMENT
Students should respect themselves, others and their environment.

VALUES STATEMENT
Behavioural management is the responsibility of the whole school community and aims to develop an environment which encourages behaviour that is caring, supportive and co-operative.

Keep, change and try

Session time: 70 minutes

Step 1 ■ Introduction
Step 2 ■ Values Scan
Step 3 ■ Critical Issues
Step 4 ■ Mission Statement
Step 5 ■ Keep, Change and Try
Step 6 ■ Key Result Areas
Step 7 ■ Focus Sheets
Step 8 ■ Pulling It Together
Step 9 ■ Client Scan (Optional)

At a Glance

Step 5 is broken into three activities or phases: keep, change and try. Participants are asked to develop a list of the key result areas that they would like to see addressed in their strategic plan. Key result areas are defined as what the organisation is doing or needs to do in order to be successful in achieving its purpose. They are the programmes, activities, policies and structures that need to be addressed.

Participants are asked first to complete a worksheet titled 'Keep'. Participants must reflect on those areas of their work where they get their best results: the areas that they personally want to ensure the school retains, even though there may be other changes.

Participants are then asked to complete a worksheet titled 'Change', in which they must identify those areas of their work that need changing in order that improvement might occur.

Next, participants complete a worksheet titled 'Try'. They are required to reflect on and discuss those areas of their work from which they get their key results and which they feel might be done differently. There may be little wrong with the present methods of doing these things, but they feel that by trying something out, there may be some improvement. From these three activities, a list of key result areas is collated.

Purpose

By this stage, the participants have spent much time thinking about their values. They have discussed and debated what they believe the school as an organisation is about, its purpose and its promise. Based on these beliefs and, in some cases, on the early input of parents through the client scans, it is now important to move on to look at the actual practices of the school and to make decisions about how these can change (or not change as the case may be) in order to position the school to take advantage of its uniqueness and environment.

The term 'key result area' is important because it is not possible (nor desirable) for participants to discuss every activity and function of the school. Rather, it is more productive to focus on those areas of their work which provide the greatest gains to themselves and the school.

The notion of 'keep' is to build on strengths, to begin with a focus on what the school and its staff are doing well. These may be the things for which the school is appreciated and which are effective. This phase is a stabilising influence in that it demonstrates a commitment to what is currently good rather than the imposition of wholesale change.

The 'change' part of the process lets participants know that they themselves are in the best position to identify what needs changing.

The 'try' phase confirms the desire for continuous improvement. Trying things out is sometimes a relatively simple and hazard-free matter; at other times, it calls for a degree of risk taking. This should be seen as an essential ingredient of an organisation that seeks to improve the way it works.

At the end of this time, the organisation should have a comprehensive list of the areas for change.

Objectives

By the end of this activity, participants will:

◆ have listed those key result areas of their work that they wish to retain;

◆ have listed as key result areas the changes that they would like to make; and

◆ have made a list of things that they would like to try out in an effort to improve their key result areas.

Making This Step Successful

In order for this step to be successful, facilitators must bear the following in mind:

◆ Participants are responsible for and proud of their input. People invariably have great ideas; it is natural for them to want to see their contributions included. They should be assured, therefore, that the final printed document will contain a listing of all the key result areas put forward by participants. Our experience shows that, for an organisation of about seventy people, the list will amount to about four pages of ideas. This is after some collation has taken place, since there will be ideas that are almost identical.

◆ Participants must know that their ideas will be treated seriously. In many cases, however, they will not be practicable for various reasons, including regulatory and financial constraints, but this should not prevent participants from airing their views. Those ideas which are accepted will have to be prioritised, and that means that while some ideas will be implemented immediately, others may have to wait a little longer.

It is worth entering a note of caution at this point. Some schools may want to shortcut the planning process by starting with the 'keep, change, try' phase, but this would be inadvisable, as it would open participants' ideas up to all sorts of motive and influence. It should be remembered that the basis of the approach is the way in which core values anchor consistency in decision making.

Directions

The facilitator should announce the following: 'This activity is about giving this school the direction and improvement it needs for the future. However, while the strategic plan will come from what you write today, we may not be able to put into effect everything we would like. Central office may not let us or we simply may not have the money. Nevertheless, I can assure you that all the ideas that you develop today will, in essence, be included in the plan'.

Step 5 ■ Phase 1 – Keep

What do participants believe, from what the school is currently doing, it should plan to keep doing into the future? What should they keep? This process takes 20 minutes.

Ask participants to describe, on the 'Keep' worksheets, the programmes, activities, policies or structures that should be retained.

The facilitator may best express the directions thus: 'Write down all the things that you want to keep whatever else happens, because they are the things about this place that are really good. They are the things that are working well. They may be the things that you know people enjoy and that you and the school are renowned for. These are the aspects of the school and your job from which you get your successes: your wins'.

When completed, individuals form groups of six to discuss those of their 'keep' ideas that they are willing to share.

All 'Keep' worksheets are collected by the facilitator for the working party to collate.

Step 5 ■ Phase 2 – Change

The 'change' phase takes 20 minutes. What do participants believe should be done differently? What should be changed over the coming months or even years?

Ask participants to describe on the 'Change' worksheets what changes they believe should be made to the programmes, activities, policies or structures, because what is currently happening could be or should be done differently to make the school more relevant, effective or efficient.

Give the following directions: 'Write down all the things you know must be changed. These are the areas of your work that you have been thinking about for a long time, because, if you had your way, they would be done differently. They are the aspects of life in school that are not working, that have passed their 'sell by' date, or that create problems for people'.

When completed, individuals form groups of six to discuss the 'change' ideas that they are willing to share.

All 'Change' worksheets are collected by the facilitator for the working party to collate.

Step 5 ■ Phase 3 – Try

The 'try' phase needs a little more time, so 30 minutes is allocated to it. Now is the opportunity to plan strategically, what innovations, ideas or new initiatives are worth trying to see if they would improve the school's ability to achieve its mission and values.

Each participant is given an index-size piece of paper on which to write an idea that they think the school should try.

Participants should *not* write their names and, if necessary, should disguise their writing.

The facilitator gives instructions as follows: 'On the piece of paper you have been given, write down an idea about something that this school should try: something that could be done differently; something new; some idea you have seen, read or heard about. The idea should be something that will improve our school's ability to achieve its purpose. Your idea will be anonymously presented. Someone else will read it out to the group, not you. Therefore, you can write down any idea. You do not have to claim ownership of it or explain it unless you want to. Your 'try' idea can be as wild, crazy or absurd as you want. Do not be constrained by what you think others expect or want to hear'.

Participants are asked to compress their papers into balls and to throw them into a collection bin in the centre of the room.

When this is completed, each participant takes out one paper from the bin.

The participants then read out the papers in turn. Participants note the ideas they like. All ideas are recorded on a 'Try' worksheet by the facilitator.

When completed, individuals form groups of six to discuss the 'try' ideas and to modify or add to some of them in order to make them workable.

Useful Advice

This 'keep, change and try' activity is always well received. This is because it provides an opportunity for people to write whatever is on their minds and then to have the idea listened to. Note that everyone is involved in the exercise, including the principal.

Worksheet 8.7

Keep

Regardless of what happens to this school in the near future, there are certain things we should keep.

A. With respect to what happens in our classrooms, we should keep …

B. With respect to our school-community relations, we should retain …

C. In our school management practices, we should keep …

D. With regard to our staff relations and development, we should keep …

Change

You have probably thought about this school and its current situation. You may have identified things that you feel need to be changed.

A. With respect to what happens in our classrooms, we should change …

B. With respect to our school-community relations, we should change …

C. In our school management practices, we should change ...

D. With regard to our staff relations and development, we should change ...

Try

For a better future for this school, what should we try out?

A. With respect to what happens in our classrooms, we should try ...

B. With respect to our school-community relations, we should try ...

C. In our school management practices, we should try ...

D. With regard to our staff relations and development, we should try ...

Keep, Change and Try: As a Client Survey Process

As an optional activity of the strategic planning process, the 'keep, change and try' session can be used as a mechanism for scanning the opinion of the broader community. For instance, various groups within the community may be invited to attend school meetings or social functions. At these meetings, the 'keep', 'change' and 'try' worksheets can be used to gather information which can be incorporated into the strategic planning process.

As an example, an urban school that services a large Greek community organised a social luncheon for parents and friends of the school. At the luncheon the 'keep', 'change' and 'try' worksheets were used (available in the Greek language also) in order to gather their views on what was good about the school, what needed changing sooner rather than later and what the school should try out.

Collating and prioritising key result areas

Session time: 30 minutes

Step 1 ■ Introduction
Step 2 ■ Values Scan
Step 3 ■ Critical Issues
Step 4 ■ Mission Statement
Step 5 ■ Keep, Change and Try
Step 6 ■ Key Result Areas
Step 7 ■ Focus Sheets
Step 8 ■ Pulling It Together
Step 9 ■ Client Scan (Optional)

At a Glance

Step 6 is where participants collate and prioritise the ideas generated during step 5. Participants are arranged into four groups, and each group is given ideas which fall under a particular heading. Thus, one group deals with classroom-related ideas, another with school-community relations, another with management practices, and the fourth group with staff relations and development.

Each group reduces the ideas to a manageable number through a process of combining or refining, and then prioritises them in the form of a ranked list.

Purpose

The collation process is an important one, since there will be too many ideas to form a workable strategic plan. Many of the ideas will be essentially similar. This is to be expected, since coffee talk often focuses on what should be done and what changes should be made.

Step 6, thus, should culminate in a workable list of key result areas which can be taken to the next step. Our experience suggests that the ideas should be reduced to a list of approximately eight to ten major key result areas.

Objectives

By the end of this step the participants will have:

- ◆ collated the ideas under each heading and reduced them to a manageable number of key result areas; and
- ◆ prioritised the resulting key result areas in the form of a ranked list.

Making This Step Successful

In order for this step to be successful:

- ◆ Participants need to understand that the previous step provided a device for thinking through ideas. Now, at this stage, we move away from the categories of 'keep', 'change' and 'try', and we focus attention on developing lists of key result areas in each of the following categories:

  classroom and what happens in it

  school-community relations

  school management practices

  staff relations and development

- ◆ Participants should work out their own ways of reducing the ideas to about eight to ten key result areas.
- ◆ This has to be done rapidly. There is insufficient time to read all the ideas aloud.

Directions

During this step the facilitator should do the following:

Arrange participants in four groups. Each group has one of the following four categories with which to deal:

classroom and what happens in it

school-community relations

school management practices

staff relations and development

Give out to the correct groups the ideas from the 'keep', 'change' and 'try' worksheets once the ideas have been cut out of the sheets. (Note that the working party will have had to operate rapidly to take the ideas from the worksheets and to separate them into the appropriate categories.)

Direct the groups to collate the ideas, producing a list of the main key result areas developed under each of the headings. These key result areas become the foci on the focus sheets in the next step of the process. Collation should combine duplicated ideas and get rid of vague or unclear ones. The process should yield eight to ten key result areas from each group.

Direct the groups to rank order the key result areas, bearing in mind that some are in need of more immediate attention than others.

Focus sheets

Session time: 120 minutes

Step 1 ■ Introduction
Step 2 ■ Values Scan
Step 3 ■ Critical Issues
Step 4 ■ Mission Statement
Step 5 ■ Keep, Change and Try
Step 6 ■ Key Result Areas
Step 7 ■ Focus Sheets
Step 8 ■ Pulling It Together
Step 9 ■ Client Scan (Optional)

At a Glance

Participants are now directed to turn ideas into something of practical utility to the school. Step 7 involves describing strategies, performance indicators, key tasks and resource implications for each key idea. The session is thus about developing a real commitment to action. While we call the documents that come out of this stage 'focus sheets', others might think of them as 'action plans'.

Purpose

The traditional strategic planner might see this as the only valid stage of the process, where the 'hard' data issues are addressed. Measurable actions and performance indicators are indeed useful, but only if they are built from organisational values.

Up to this point, participants have scanned values, developed a mission and spent time making suggestions about what should be kept, changed and tried in their work. They should now be more than ready to commit themselves to making these plans happen.

There are two important purposes served by the focus sheets. They are:

♦ *An Acid Test.* When formulating their ideas in the 'keep, change and try' step, participants were encouraged to think laterally, to obtain ideas from wherever they could think of, and to be generally unconstrained in what they saw as the best way to improve the key result areas of their work and the school's achievements. This process may have resulted in some ideas that were unworkable. One of the major purposes of the focus sheets is to get the participants to see that some of their ideas will not work. This is achieved by the expedient method of asking them to say how their ideas can be put into operation.

♦ *A Commitment.* For those staff who have up to this point been sceptical about the use of such a planning process, the development of focus sheets is a sign of commitment. If participants can write up their ideas in the form of practical actions, then it is these actions (expressed as performance indicators and strategies) that will test the rhetoric of management.

Objectives

By the end of this stage, the participants will:

♦ have taken their ideas and developed them into action plans;

♦ have written strategies for each key idea;

♦ have written performance indicators for each key idea;

♦ have written key tasks that describe who is responsible for actions; and

♦ have considered the resource implications.

Making This Step Successful

The facilitator should note the following points:

♦ The importance of these focus sheets as plans of action must be emphasised. If anyone wants to have a real say and to make changes, then just having an idea is simply not good enough. He or she must answer questions about who, where, when and how. That ensures that the idea is workable and if it is not adopted, the author would have the right to an explanation.

◆ Participants need to develop some skill in writing performance indicators.

◆ Participants should write focus sheets in groups of two or three people. It is difficult to write them in isolation, since a critical colleague is required to test out the validity of performance indicators and the efficiency of key tasks.

◆ All focus sheets must be collected, including those that are incomplete. The next step involves processing and prioritising these plans of action.

Directions

During this step the facilitator should do the following:

Arrange the participants in pairs or groups of three. Allow people to select their own partners based on whom they would normally work with in school.

Distribute the blank focus sheets, plus an example of a completed focus sheet to give them an idea of how it should be done. This is shown as a worksheet.

Direct participants to choose one of the key result areas ideas from one of the 'keep', 'change' and 'try' worksheets, and to write it in the space titled Key Result Area.

Direct participants to write a strategy or strategic goal for the key result area. A strategy is described as one of the possible ways in which the key result area can be put into action. It is worded as a goal or objective.

Direct participants to write at least one performance indicator for the strategy. Performance indicators can be based on final outcomes (the end product) or on process outputs (signs of action during the process of doing). Performance indicators must include a date and an action and, where possible, should be empirically demonstrable.

Instruct participants to show how indicators can be achieved through the use of key tasks. These are to include the names of people (or positions), actions and dates.

Ask the participants to consider and list financial and other resource implications. These should include sources of funding and workload for staff.

Direct the working party to collate the focus sheets. Participants should label each sheet according to the classifications provided.

Useful Advice

This stage of the process is usually without problems. Participants are informed that they are being asked to take their ideas and to make them workable. They are invariably able to develop strategies, performance indicators and key tasks that make the operationalisation of their ideas possible. They can develop focus sheets on single key result area ideas in 20 minutes.

It needs to be clarified that they are not expected to write a focus sheet for every key result area. The planning process provides general directions and does not list every possible action or outcome.

One concern commonly raised by participants is, what is the difference between a strategic goal and a key result area statement?

Answer: There can be many different strategic goals that need to be accomplished in each key result area. Strategic goals are simply a way of defining action goals that are one level lower or more specific than key result areas. For example, a key result area might focus on *the development of improved parent-teacher communication.*

To achieve this, there can be many strategic goals:

To establish a home liaison officer post.

To increase parent involvement on the school management committees.

To encourage teachers to contact parents directly about student counselling and welfare matters.

Worksheet 8.8

Focus Sheet

_____ (Focus)

Key result area	
Strategy (strategic goal)	
Performance indicator (output or outcome)	
Key tasks (action, who, when)	
Resources/ funding source	

EXAMPLE

(Focus) Professional Development

Key result area	Improved communication and collaborative input to decision making at all levels of decision making.
Strategy (strategic goal)	As we believe this to be a two-way process, all staff to be involved in professional development designed to improve communication and collaboration skills.
Performance indicator (output or outcome)	By December 1998: All staff to have attended at least 4 hours of school based in-service activity on some of the following: communication, conflict, collaborative school processes.
Key tasks (action, who, when)	• Professional Development (PD) Committee to investigate possible in-service providers by March 1998. • PD Committee to investigate possible in-house staff to conduct programmes, where possible, by March 1998. • School Council to investigate possibility of parental involvement in in-service programme by December 1998. • Deputy Head to establish task committee to investigate involvement of student body in decision making workshops by March 1998.
Resources/ funding source	To be determined by PD Committee.

Performance Indicator Writing

In writing the focus sheets, it is often necessary to conduct a short instructional session on how to write performance indicators. The following notes may be useful.

There are two types of performance indicator which are useful to educators: those that measure the outcome at the end of a programme and those which show you that you are actually making progress towards achieving your desired ends.

Values based strategic planning is an ongoing process; the performance indicators we need, therefore, are those that enable us to see how well we are progressing. It is not good enough to wait until the end of the plan to see if any difference was made to the school.

Outcome indicators demonstrate the extent to which the goals have been met. These are effectiveness indicators that usually provide a measure of the specific objectives to be achieved at the end of the programme.

Output indicators, on the other hand, demonstrate that action has been undertaken and usually give an indication of the outward features of a programme in operation. Output indicators are vital, because they are signposts of success or celebration points along the way.

Some Helpful Hints for Writing Outcome and Output Indicators

Using the right language is important when writing performance indicators. Jeffery (1991) suggests the following:

♦   To determine the appropriate performance indicator for a particular programme outcome, ask the question 'How will I know when the problem is solved?' Then begin the answer with the phrase 'By the extent to which ...'

♦   To determine the appropriate performance indicator for a particular programme output, ask the question 'What outward features will tell me that action has been taken?' Then begin the answer with the phrase 'By the extent of ...'

All performance indicators, both outcome and output, should be in some way tangible or measurable; that is, performance indicators need to be worded in such a way that they can be judged to have happened and to what extent they have occurred.

For example: A performance indicator might be
By the extent to which ...

All staff have attended at least 4 hours of workplace based in-service activity on at least one of the following topics: communication, team building, work improvement groups.

Target date: December 1998

This is a performance indicator because, by the review date, it would be possible to determine if indeed all staff had been to 4 hours of in-service activity (or what percentage of the staff had done so) and on what topics.

Pulling it together

Session time: 20 minutes

Step 1 ■ Introduction
Step 2 ■ Values Scan
Step 3 ■ Critical Issues
Step 4 ■ Mission Statement
Step 5 ■ Keep, Change and Try
Step 6 ■ Key Result Areas
Step 7 ■ Focus Sheets
Step 8 ■ Pulling It Together
Step 9 ■ Client Scan (Optional)

At a Glance

At the end of the session, when the groups have completed their focus sheets, the facilitator needs to summarise the day, show how everything is linked and reinforce how much has been achieved.

At this time, a strategic plan working party needs to be identified. This group is charged with assembling the final document from what has been produced during the session. The working party has two things to do:

◆ It has to gather together the value statements, the mission statement, the key result areas and the focus sheets. Then it has to put all that material into a draft plan for circulation to all participants.

◆ It then has to produce the final working version in the form of an attractive document which can be distributed to the wider public. It is worth investing in a professional job so that participants will be proud to see their work included.

Purpose

In the values-based approach, it is the process that is important so that those involved can become the driving forces for change. While an attractive, glossy document is good to have, it does not serve much use if the first people know about it is when it arrives on their desks or through the post. In values based strategic planning, the document is the temporary culmination of much hard work by many people and one that reminds everyone of their commitment to the future of their school.

Objectives

By the end of this step:

◆ a working party will have been formed;

◆ it will have collected all the work produced during the planning process; and

◆ it will have used professional expertise to produce an attractive strategic plan.

Making This Step Successful

In order to ensure that this step is successful:

◆ the working party should comprise staff from different levels of the school and community members, and should include the principal where possible;

◆ during the 20 minutes allocated for this session, all written worksheets produced during the strategic planning process should be collected and labelled clearly.

Directions

The facilitator should ensure that:

◆ a working party of five to six people is formed;

◆ the working party comprises a good mix of people;

♦ all written papers and worksheets are collected and clearly labelled;

♦ all participants understand that the working party is responsible for editing their contributions and perhaps sequencing the ideas, but that it will not reject the participants' ideas or plans.

Useful Advice

The strategic plan should contain a brief overview of the process, the values, the mission, the critical issues, the key result areas and all the focus sheets developed by participants, rewritten for consistency and style.

The final act of the planning event is to bring the meeting to a close. The principal or chair of the school's council should say a few congratulatory words to participants and should assure them that their contributions will have a significant impact on the school. It is a good idea to end the event with a short social activity including refreshments.

But first, a review date must be set. The purpose of the review date is to ensure that the planning activities are carried out as described in the focus sheets. The review date also signifies the point at which the next strategic planning process should begin. In values based strategic planning, the end of one cycle is merely the start of the next. The end of the planning process is not an evaluation as such, but a review, the focus of which is to look forward to the next planning cycle.

Questions to be asked in the review might include:

♦ Have the performance indicators that were set by participants not been achieved because of a shift in the environment or because of staff changes?

♦ Have the school's values shifted?

♦ Has the mission statement changed?

♦ Has the relationship with the community changed?

♦ Who should now be involved in the planning process?

The working party is responsible for setting up the review, and this should normally take place about six months to one year after this planning event.

We have mentioned the word 'evaluation'. There is, of course, a direct link between the evaluation of performance and strategic planning. If, as we have suggested, 'strategic' means positioning the organisation to take best advantage of its situation, then it involves a specific view about the role of evaluation. Evaluation must be seen as a device for improving performance: it must thus adopt a developmental focus.

The view that evaluation is about monitoring performance to maintain standards at set levels is incongruent with values based strategic planning. There is no such thing as ensuring that the school's problems are 'fixed'. Strategic planning must be seen as a process for improving what the school is doing. It is about changing things so that what is valued by the school and its community can be reflected in practice and so that improvement might be continuous.

Client scan

Step 1 ■ Introduction
Step 2 ■ Values Scan
Step 3 ■ Critical Issues
Step 4 ■ Mission Statement
Step 5 ■ Keep, Change and Try
Step 6 ■ Key Result Areas
Step 7 ■ Focus Sheets
Step 8 ■ Pulling It Together
Step 9 ■ Client Scan (Optional)

At a Glance

The client scan is an optional process that is not used very often. Client scanning is recommended only if parents and other community members are not involved in the strategic planning process as direct participants.

The process of scanning we recommend does not involve sending long and complex questionnaires to people's homes, but is based on the principle that making contact with members of the community by phone to let them know that you are interested in their input is highly effective.

Each member of the teaching staff is asked to phone five parents and to ask them a prepared list of questions that should take no longer than 3 minutes. This scanning process is designed to make first contact with parents. Such contact will provide only a limited amount of information, but it may encourage parents to give more detailed information, either in writing or during a personal visit to the school. If teachers wish, they may make visits to parents' homes in situations where this is acceptable practice.

Purpose

The client scanning process in this programme is only the first part of the overall inquiry into the needs of parents and the community. The second part of the process of inquiry occurs in the 'keep, change and try' stage.

The phone scan serves two purposes: first, it ensures that the process of seeking client input involves all the staff of the school and is not left solely in the hands of the executive or community liaison officers. It thus brings teachers into productive contact with parents. It is good for parents to be asked by teachers for views, as the teacher–parent relationship is usually very different in nature. Some teachers may actually champion parents' opinions.

Second, while a 3-minute phone survey may elicit some useful information, the initial contact serves to break the ice and to encourage more extended dialogue in the future.

Objectives

By the end of this activity, participants will:

♦ know how to conduct a 3-minute phone survey of parents or other community members;

♦ have been given instruction on how to follow up the interview by sending out the responses to parents and inviting them to send in more information;

♦ agree to phone five parents; and

♦ agree to incorporate any input they receive from parents or community members in future planning activities.

Making This Step Successful

In order for this step to be successful:

♦ teachers must feel comfortable in phoning parents; it helps therefore to have a demonstration;

◆ there must be easy access to phones for teachers, and it must be shown how to keep the call short;

◆ teachers must understand that parents like to be asked for their views; this makes the relationship positive; and

◆ the teachers should have a scripted set of questions.

Directions

Facilitators begin by demonstrating a poor phone conversation. This should involve two role players. This should be done with humour.

Without explanation, the two role-playing facilitators should change roles and immediately begin a second role play, this time a good phone conversation, demonstrating that the process can take just 3 minutes and is actually welcomed by the parent. The questions must be displayed on a transparency while the conversation is taking place.

The final part of the role play should demonstrate that a copy of the questions and the responses are sent to the parent with an enclosed pre-addressed envelope inviting further comment.

At the end of the second role play, teachers should be invited to discuss what they have seen demonstrated.

Prompt questions for this discussion can include:

◆ How often do parents get called by teachers if their children are not in trouble?

◆ Do you think that parents would like to talk about the school if given the opportunity?

◆ If you are a parent, would such a call from the teachers of your children bother you?

◆ How can parents make confidential comments when you are talking to them on the phone?

◆ What do you do with the comments of parents when you have them?

After the discussion, direct participants to work in pairs to write a 3-minute script of the questions they would ask their parents.

Select pairs at random to demonstrate their questions. It is possible to set up demonstration interviews and to time them to ensure that they fall within the time frame suggested.

Discuss how teachers will select which parents they will call.

The Wall

The 'Wall' is basically a mobile notice board or pin board that can be taken from one location to another. Community members are invited to stick notes on the board with their comments and opinions about the school and its operation. To start it off, comments from well-known community personnel might be put on the board for everyone to read. Parents and community members can add their comments. It should be cleared frequently, and sometimes support can be provided for those without an adequate level of English proficiency.

In assisting a school in a small rural community to develop a strategic plan, we proposed the use of a Wall, because the majority of parents were of Aboriginal descent; in this area of the country they would normally have little contact with the school or its staff. Past attempts by the school to involve parents had all been to no avail. For example, so few parents had turned up to parent–teacher nights that the school had moved them to afternoons, then to Saturdays, and had then given up altogether. Letters home were seldom answered, and school social events had been failures.

The Wall was a large piece of framed square Masonite (two metres wide and one metre high) built by the senior woodwork class and painted in the school's colours by the janitor. It had two cups in which were placed pencils and adhesive pads.

The Wall, on its first outing, was taken by two of the school's teachers and the community liaison officer to the local shopping centre. A large sign was placed next to the Wall, and the community liaison officer and teachers stayed with the Wall on a roster system all day. By the end of that first day, few messages had been posted on the Wall. Unshaken, the staff returned to the Wall the following day (which coincided with government pay day). This time, the staff left the Wall unattended during the lunch time rush and for an hour in the morning and three hours in the afternoon.

The community liaison officer had arranged for four of her close friends to write messages and stick them on the Wall during the first of these unattended sessions. The messages snowballed. By the end of the second day, the staff took over twenty-six messages from the Wall.

By the end of the week, over sixty-five different comments and messages had been placed legitimately on the Wall. By the end of that week, parents had the confidence to approach the staff and ask them to write messages for them.

While the Wall attracted a small number of obscene comments (these were removed when noticed), the majority of comments, especially by the end of the week, were legitimate and were highly valued by the school. One of the most frequent comments actually led to major changes in the operation of the school's timetable in the following semester. Another led to an investigation into the operation of the school canteen.

Useful Advice

Initially teachers are sceptical about being involved in phoning parents. Contact between parents and teachers may occur only if something is wrong or on parent–teacher interview nights.

It is important to ensure:

◆ that teachers can practise their calls;

◆ that teachers realise the process takes a minimal amount of time;

◆ that teachers recognise their contact will be received positively; and

◆ that the call is to act merely as the first contact.

Worksheets

The example given is merely to show how simple the questions can be, but it is best not to use a common instrument, since there is much to be gained from the diversity in individually designed question sheets. Furthermore, individuals can base their questions on key values, and even the same values can throw up vastly different questions.

The sheet entitled 'Client Scan Questions from Value Statements' can be given out to teachers and used to help them formulate their questions. At the same time, they can be given a blank form like the worksheet shown next. In pairs, they write questions that are related to the value statements which have been agreed are representative of the school's values. Time is too short to write a question for each value, so each pair should decide which values to use based on their own preferences.

Worksheet 8.9

Example of Phone Scan Survey Script

Teacher: _____ Dept.: _____

(1) Is your child happy to be at this school?

    5   4   3   2   1

    Where 5 is very happy and 1 is not happy at all.

(2) As part of our belief in caring for students' achievements, we try to provide a comprehensive report to parents every ten weeks. Is this helpful?

    5   4   3   2   1

    Where 5 is very helpful and 1 is not helpful at all.

(3) How would you rate the attitude of the people you deal with in this school?

    5   4   3   2   1

    Where 5 is very helpful and 1 is not helpful at all.

(4) Do you have any suggestions about ways in which we could change how we operate? Are there any other services that you think we should provide?

_____

_____

_____

_____

_____

Send copy of questions to (parent's name):

Address/fax number:

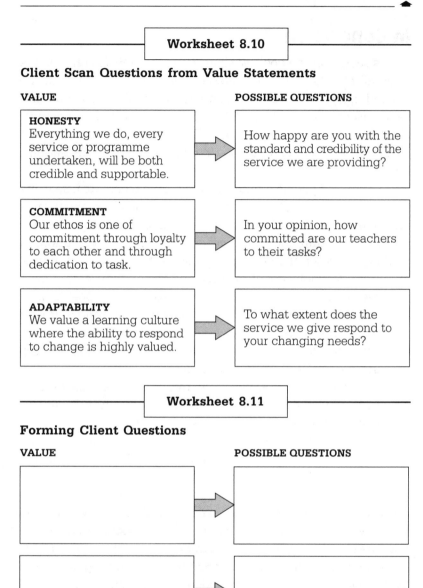

Worksheet 8.10

Client Scan Questions from Value Statements

VALUE	POSSIBLE QUESTIONS
HONESTY Everything we do, every service or programme undertaken, will be both credible and supportable.	How happy are you with the standard and credibility of the service we are providing?
COMMITMENT Our ethos is one of commitment through loyalty to each other and through dedication to task.	In your opinion, how committed are our teachers to their tasks?
ADAPTABILITY We value a learning culture where the ability to respond to change is highly valued.	To what extent does the service we give respond to your changing needs?

Worksheet 8.11

Forming Client Questions

VALUE	POSSIBLE QUESTIONS

In Conclusion

In this section of the book, we have gone through the finer points of detail of values based strategic planning. The steps can be applied in any school and indeed in many other types of organisation. However, it will be evident that there has to be a commitment from senior management to 'letting go', to accepting that all have a significant part to play in influencing the organisation's future.

A strategic plan is a process, and that is where its true value lies. It is not so much about the document itself or about aims and objectives, but about people working together to seek a greater understanding of themselves and their organisation. In working together, they discover some of the values that anchor important decisions about purpose and intent; they learn how to improve their work practices; they develop a relationship with the recipients of the service with a view to generating a greater understanding of need and expectation; and they systematically develop plans which lead to continuous improvement and which demand a commitment from all concerned.

A strategic plan developed in this way is of considerable benefit to the school and the people who work in it. It enables the school to take the best advantage of its situation, resources and staff abilities. Seen in this light, it makes sense that the people who should formulate it are those with a stake in the organisation.

This book cannot end without a word to organisational leaders about their role in the values-based process. The process – and this may come as a surprise to some – demands strong leadership. It is true that it is an empowering approach which provokes wide involvement, but this, strangely enough, empowers organisational leaders all the more. And this makes them strong. It is indeed a test of leadership to value employees and to value their contributions. It is even more demanding to involve those who are outside the institution. In promoting participation, high-order people skills, communication and conflict resolution skills are needed to overcome the open scepticism and cynicism that may be displayed by employees who have in the past been subjected to 'mission by imposition'.

For some, this is too much to bear and they gravitate to the typical practices of weak leaders: issuing edicts and planning in isolation. Commitment from others, for them, is illusory. Sadly, such leaders belong to a bygone age. They are anachronisms. The organisational world in which we now work is a vastly different one to the past. The high-demand leaders are those who draw on and co-ordinate the value which their people bring to the organisation.

If you were to ask a school principal or the chief of any organisation where their greatest assets lie, the answer would invariably refer to the people in the organisation. We would go one step further and say the answer is all people associated with the organisation, including employees, clients and all those with a genuine interest or stake in the organisation. Now, imagine, if you could share in the knowledge and ideas that they all possess, you would have a wealth of information and wisdom which could form the basis for transformational change. Values based strategic planning does precisely that: it draws on the knowledge, experience and wisdom of all those associated with the organisation, and brings these together in such a way that the people's commitment to improvement and success can be assured and in such a form that the organisation can be positioned to face an uncertain, sometimes daunting, but vibrantly challenging future.

References

Achilles, C. (1987). 'A vision of better schools'. In W. Greenfield (ed.). *Instructional Leadership: Concepts, Issues and Controversies*. New York: Cassell.

Angus, L. (1989). 'New leadership and the possibilities of educational reform'. In J. Smyth (ed.). *Critical Perspectives on Educational Leadership*. New York: The Falmer Press.

Angus, L. (1995). 'Cultural theory in educational administration'. In C. Evers and J. Chapman (eds.). *Educational Administration: An Australian Perspective*. St Leonards, NSW: Allen and Unwin.

Argyris, C. and D. Schon (1978). *Organisational Learning: A Theory of Action Perspective*. Reading, MA: Addison Wesley.

Bajunid, I.A. (1996). 'Preliminary explorations of indigenous perspectives of educational management: The evolving Malaysian experience'. *Journal of Educational Administration*, Vol. 34, No. 5, pp. 50–73.

Bates, R. (1982). *Educational Administration, the Sociology of Science, and the Management of Knowledge*. Geelong: Deakin University Press.

Beck, C. (1993). *Learning to Live the Good Life*. Toronto: OISE Press.

Begley, P. (1996). 'Cognitive perspectives on values in administration: A quest for coherence and relevance'. *Educational Administration Quarterly*, Vol. 32, No. 3, pp. 403–426.

Begley, P. and K. Leithwood (1990). 'The influence of values on school administrator practices'. *Journal of Personnel Evaluation in Education*, Vol. 3, pp. 337–352.

Bhindi, N. and P. Duignan (1996). 'Leadership 2020: A visionary paradigm'. Paper presented at the Eighth International Conference of the

Commonwealth Council for Educational Administration, Kuala Lumpur, Malaysia, 19–24 August.

Bloor, G. and P. Davidson (1994). 'Understanding professional culture in organisational context'. *Organization Studies*, Vol. 15, No. 2, pp. 50–69.

Bolman, L. and T. Deal (1991). *Reframing Organisations*. San Francisco: Jossey-Bass.

Bryson, J.M. (1989). *Strategic Planning for Public and Non-profit Organisations: A Guide to Strengthening and Sustaining Organisational Achievement*. London: Jossey-Bass.

Burns, J. (1978). *Leadership*. New York: Harper and Row.

Burrell, G. and G. Morgan (1979). *Sociological Paradigms and Organisational Analysis: Elements of the Sociology of Corporate Life*. London: Heinemann.

Caldwell, B. (1994). 'Leading the transformation of Australia's schools'. *Educational Management and Administration*, Vol. 22, No. 2, pp. 76–84.

Caldwell, B. and J. Spinks (1988). *The Self-Managing School*. London: The Falmer Press.

Caldwell, B. and J. Spinks (1992). *Leading the Self-Managing School*. London: The Falmer Press.

Campbell-Evans, G. (1993). 'A values perspective on school-based management'. In C. Dimmock (ed.). *School-Based Management and School Effectiveness*. London: Routledge.

Carr, D. and I. Littman (1990). *Excellence in Government – Total Quality Management in the 1990s*. Arlington, VA: Coopers and Lybrand.

Chantico Series, The (1989). *Strategic and Operational Planning for Information Systems*. Wellesley, MA: QED Information Sciences Inc.

Chapman, J. and C. Evers (1995). *Educational Administration: An Australian Perspective*. St Leonards, NSW: Allen & Unwin.

Cheng, K.M. and K. Wong (1996). 'School effectiveness in East Asia: Concepts, origins and implications'. *Journal of Educational Administration*, Vol. 34, No. 5, pp. 32–49.

Cheng, Y.C. (1995). 'School effectiveness and improvement in Hong Kong, Taiwan and mainland China'. *ICSEI Country Reports*. Friesland, Netherlands: Gemeenschappelijk Centrun Onderwijsbegeleiding.

Codd, J. (1984). *Philosophy, Common Sense, and Action in Educational Administration*. Geelong: Deakin University Press.

Covey, S. (1992). *Principle Centered Leadership*. New York: Simon & Schuster.

Cutterance, P. (1995). 'Quality assurance and quality management in education'. In C. Evers and J. Chapman (eds.). *Educational Administration: An Australian Perspective*. St Leonards, NSW: Allen & Unwin.

Davies, G., P. Weller and C. Lewis (1989). *Corporate Management in Australian Government*. Melbourne: Macmillan.

Department of Education (1992). *Formulation of an Annual School Plan*. Hong Kong: Advisory Committee on the School Management Initiative, Hong Kong Education Department, Hong Kong Government Printers.

Dimmock, C. and A. Walker (1997). 'Comparative educational administration: Developing across cultural conceptual framework'. Paper prepared at the Chinese University of Hong Kong, Hong Kong.

Dimmock, C. and A. Walker (1998, in press). 'Towards comparative educational administration: The case for a cross-cultural, school based approach'. *Journal of Educational Administration*, Vol. 36, No. 2.

Duignan, P. and R. MacPherson (1991). *Educative Leadership Project Series*. Canberra ACT: ACT Ministry of Education.

Edinborough, T. (1994). 'Planning for quality'. In P. Ribbins and E. Burridge (eds.). *Improving Education Promoting Quality in Schools*. London: Cassell.

Education Commission (1996). *Education Commission Report No. 7 (ECR7). Quality School Education*. Hong Kong: The Government Printer.

Foster, W.P. (1980). 'Administration and the crisis in legitimacy: A review of Habermsian thought'. *Harvard Educational Review*, Vol. 50, No. 4, pp. 496–505.

Fullan, M. (1993). *Change Forces: Probing the Depths of Educational Reform*. New York: The Falmer Press.

Garmston, R. and B. Wellman (1995). 'Adaptive schools in a quantum universe'. *Educational Leadership*, Vol. 52, No. 7, pp. 6–14.

Giddens, A. (1984). *The Constitution of Society*. Cambridge: Polity Press.

Giroux, H. (1989). *Critical Theory and Educational Practice*. Geelong: Deakin University Press.

Glatter, R. (1988). 'The management of school improvement'. In R. Glatter, M. Preedy, C. Rickes and M. Masterton (eds.). *Understanding School Management*. Milton Keynes: Open University Press.

Greenfield, T. (1975). 'Theory about organisation: A new perspective and its implications for schools'. In V. Houghton et al. (eds.). *Management in Education*, Vol. 1. London: Ward Lock Educational.

Greenfield, T. (1980). 'The man who came back through the Door in the

Wall: Discovering the truth, discovering self, discovering organisations'. *Educational Administration Quarterly*, Vol. 6, No. 3, pp. 25–59.

Greenfield, T. (1986). 'The decline and fall of science in educational administration'. *Interchange*, Vol. 17, No. 1, pp. 57–80.

Greer, J. and P. Short (1994). 'Restructuring schools'. In L. Hughes (ed.). *The Principal as Leader.* New York: Merrill.

Hallinger, P. (1987). 'Educational leadership ASEAN 2000'. Paper delivered to the first ASEAN Asian Symposium on Educational Management and Leadership IAB Malaysia.

Hallinger, P. and K. Leithwood (1996). 'Culture and educational administration: A case of finding out what you do not know you do not know'. *Journal of Educational Administration*, Vol. 34, No. 5, pp. 98–116.

Hammer, M. and S. Stanton (1995). *The Reengineering Revolution: A Handbook.* Sydney: HarperCollins.

Hargreaves, A. (1994). *Changing Teachers, Changing Times.* New York: Cassell.

Hargreaves, D. and D. Hopkins (1991). *The Empowered School.* London: Cassell.

Herman, J.L. and J.J. Herman (1995). 'Defining administrative tasks, evaluation performing and developing skills'. *NASSP Bulletin*, Vol. 79, No. 567, pp. 16–21.

Hodgkinson, C. (1978). *Towards a Philosophy of Administration.* Oxford: Basil Blackwell.

Hofstede, G.H. (1994). 'Cultural constraints in management theories'. *International Review of Strategic Management*, Vol. 5, pp. 27–48.

Hutchinson, B. and P. Whitehouse (1986). 'Action research, professional competence and school organisation'. *British Educational Research Journal*, Vol. 12, No. 1, pp. 85–94.

Ingram, B. (1992). *Teacher Appraisal Cycle.* Christchurch: User Friendly Resource Enterprises Ltd.

Jeffery, N. (1991). 'Demonstrating accountability in the school library: The role of performance indicators'. *Access*, Vol. 5, No. 3.

Kaufman, R. (1992). *Strategic Planning Plus: An Organisational Guide.* London: SGE Publications.

Kaufman, R. and J. Herman (1991). *Strategic Planning in Education: Rethinking, Restructuring, Revitalizing.* Lancaster, PA: Technomic Publishing Co.

Keidel, R. (1994). 'Rethinking organisational design'. *Academy of Management Executive*, Vol. 8, No. 4.

Kiggundu, M. (1989). *Managing Organizations in Developing Countries: An Operational and Strategic Approach.* Connecticut: Kumarian Press Inc.

Lakomski, G. and C. Evers (1995). 'Theory in educational administration'. In C. Evers and J. Chapman (eds.). *Educational Administration: An Australian Perspective.* St Leonards, NSW: Allen & Unwin.

Langhorne, P. (1992, April). 'Rationalisation – The importance of human resource management in a time of change'. Paper from the Sydney University, Australian Investment Conference.

Leithwood, K. (1992). 'The move towards transformational leadership'. *Educational Leadership*, Vol. 49, No. 5, pp. 8–12.

Leithwood, K., P. Begley and J. Cousins (1994). *Developing Expert Leadership for Future Schools.* London: The Falmer Press.

Leithwood, K. and D. Musella (1991). *Understanding School System Administration.* London: The Falmer Press.

Lieberman, A. and L. Miller (1990). 'Restructuring schools: What really matters, what works'. *Phi Delta Kappa*, Vol. 71, No. 10, pp. 759–764.

MacGilchrist, B., P. Mortimore, J. Savage and C. Beresford (1995). *Planning Matters: The Impact of Development Planning in Primary Schools.* London: Paul Chapman Publishing.

Macpherson, R. (1996). 'The third watershed in building theories of educational administration: Implications for indigenous research and leadership practice'. Paper presented at the Eighth International Conference of the Commonwealth Council for Educational Administration, Kuala Lumpur, Malaysia, 19–24 August.

Martinsons, M. (1996). 'Michael Hammer meets Confucius: Re-engineering Chinese business processes'. *The Hong Kong Manager*, May/June, pp. 6–17.

Ministry of Education (1987). 'Towards excellence in schools, a report to the minister'. Singapore: Singapore National Printers.

Mintzberg, H. (1994). *The Rise and Fall of Strategic Planning.* New York: Prentice Hall.

Morgan, G. (1997). *Images of Organisation* (Revised Edition). London: Sage Publications.

Mortimore, P. (1996a). 'Partnership and co-operation in school improvement'. Paper presented at the Association for Teacher Education in Europe Conference, Glasgow, Scotland.

Mortimore, P. (1996b). 'The school as a community of learners'. *Leading and Managing*, Vol. 2, No. 4, pp. 251–266.

O'Donoghue, T. and C. Dimmock (1996). 'School development planning and classroom teachers: A Western Australian case-study'. *School Organisation*, Vol. 16, pp. 71–78.

Pascale, P. (1990). *Managing the Edge*. New York: Touchstone.

Patterson, J. (1993). *Leadership for Tomorrow's Schools*. Alexandria, VA: ASCD.

Pedler, M., J. Burgoyne and T. Boydell (1991). *The Learning Company*. Maidenhead: McGraw-Hill.

Radford, M., L. Mann, Y. Ohta and Y. Nakane (1993). 'Differences between Australian and Japanese students in decisional self-esteem, decisional stress, and coping styles'. *Journal of Cross-Cultural Psychology*, Vol. 24, No. 3, pp. 284–297.

Rost, J. (1991). *Leadership for the 21st Century*. New York: Praeger.

Saul, P. (1987). 'Change: The strategic human resource management challenges'. In R. Stone (ed.). *Readings in Human Resource Management*. Sydney: John Wiley and Sons.

Schlechty, P. (1991). *Schools for the 21st Century: Leadership Imperatives for Educational Reform*. New York: Jossey-Bass.

Schon, D. (1983). *The Reflective Practitioner*. London: Temple Smith.

Schon, D. (1990). 'Dynamic conservatism'. In D. Pettit, P. Duignan and R. Macpherson (eds.). *Educative Leadership and Reorganising the Delivery of Educational Services*. Canberra, ACT: ACT Schools Authority.

Scott, R. (1991). 'Policy making and the senior educational executive'. In F. Crowther and D. Ogilvie (eds.). *The New Political World of Educational Administration*. Hawthorn, Vic: Australian Council for Educational Administration.

Semler, R. (1993). *Maverick!* London: Century.

Senge, P. (1990). *The Fifth Discipline: The Art and Practice of the Learning Organization*. New York: Doubleday.

Sergiovanni, T. (1995). *The Principalship: A Reflective Practice Perspective* (3rd Edition). Boston: Allyn and Bacon.

Simon, H. (1965). *Administrative Behaviour* (2nd Edition). New York: Free Press.

Smith, J. and J. Blase (1991). 'From empiricism to hermeneutics: Educational leadership as a practical and moral activity'. *Journal of Educational Administration*, Vol. 29, No. 1, pp. 6–21.

Smyth, J., ed. (1989). *Critical Perspectives on Educational Leadership*. London: The Falmer Press.

Smyth, J. (1992). 'Teachers' work and the politics of reflection'. *American Educational Research Journal*, Vol. 29, No. 2, pp. 267–300.

Smyth, J. (1993). *A Socially Critical View of the Self-Managing School*. London: The Falmer Press.

Stacey, R. (1991). *The Chaos Frontier: Creative Strategic Control for Business*. Oxford: Butterworth-Heinemann.

Stacey, R. (1993). *Strategic Management and Organisational Dynamics*. London: Pitman.

Starratt, R. (1993). *Transforming Life in Schools*. Melbourne: Australian Council for Educational Administration.

Stoll, L. (1992). 'Teacher growth in effective schools'. In M. Fullan, M. Hargreaves and A. Hargreaves (eds.). *Teacher Development and Educational Change*. London: The Falmer Press.

Stott, K. and A. Walker (1992). 'The nature and use of mission statements'. *Educational Management and Administration*, Vol. 20, No. 1, pp. 49–57.

Stott, K. and A. Walker (1995). *Teams, Teamwork and Teambuilding: The Manager's Complete Guide to Teams in Organisations*. Singapore: Prentice Hall.

Strong, J. (1994). *The Australian Way*, Qantas Airline Magazine, 1–2 November.

Tierney, W. (1996). 'Leadership and postmodernism: On voice and qualitative method'. *Leadership Studies*, Vol. 7, No. 3, pp. 371–383.

Villa, R. and J. Thousand, eds. (1995). 'The rationales for creating inclusive schools'. In *Creating an Inclusive School*. Alexandria, VA: ASCD.

Walker, A., E. Bridges and B. Chan (1996). 'Wisdom gained, wisdom given: Instituting PBL in a Chinese culture'. *Journal of Educational Administration*, Vol. 34, No. 5, pp. 12–31.

Walker, A. and K. Quong (1998, in press). 'Valuing difference for dealing with tensions of educational leadership in a global society'. *Peabody Journal of Education* (USA).

Walker, A. and J. Walker (1998, in press). 'Challenging the boundaries of sameness: Leadership through valuing difference'. *Journal of Educational Administration*, Vol. 36, No. 1.

Walker, B. (1994). 'Valuing differences: The concept and a model'. In C. Mabey and P. Iles (eds.). *Managing Learning*. London: Open University Press.

Whiteley, A. (1995). *Managing Change: A Core Values Approach*. South Melbourne: Macmillan Education.

Index

absentee reporting programme, 88, 89–90

accountability, 7, 25, 51, 98, 102, 105, 116

achievement elements, 46

action plans, 9, 10, 26, 29, 33, 69, 86, 138, 141, 146, 194
see also focus sheets

adaptive learning, 64

administration and values, 97–9, 125, 126

administrative science, traditional, 66, 74

affective elements, 45–6

Angus, L., 107

Annual School Plans, 26–7

Argyris, C., 65

Asian values, 97

assessment, 29

assumptions, 37

At a glance (planning session steps), 153, 158–9, 165, 168, 172–3, 174–5, 178–9, 183–4, 190, 193, 201–2, 205–6

audits
of environment, 139
of performance, *see* performance audits

of programmes, 100, 101

Austrade, 113

Australia
expressed values case study from, 121–2
reengineering in, 55, 56–7
self-managing schools in, 24, 25
strategic planning requirements in, 27
use of The Wall in, 208–9

autonomy, 25, 53, 105

Bajunid, I.A., 97–8

Beck, C., 107

Begley, P., 98, 101, 102

beliefs, *see* values and beliefs

benchmarks, 137

best practice, 19, 100, 101, 112

big picture planning, 14

Bolman, L., 70–1

bottom-up decisions, 74, 159, 162

Boydell, T., 64

bribes, 69

Bryson, J.M., 16, 31, 81

budgets, 57

Burgoyne, J., 64

Burns, J., 103

business plans, 9, 88, 89–90

Caldwell, B., 25–6
Canadian self-managing schools, 24
careers, 123–4
censorship, social, 127
central requirements and school values, 126–30
chalk-face planning, 14, 16
Chan, Dr J., 5, 17, 43
Chang, P., 81–2
change
  grassroots, 77
  leaders and, 63
  planning and, 8–9, 174
  predictability of, 174
  resistance to, 5, 6, 91, 131
  school governance and, 8
  stakeholders' demands for, 54
  strategic plan driven, 23, 50
  strategic planning practice and, 43, 44–6
  strategic thinking and, 80
  teaching staff and, 23, 46, 131
  top-down imposition and, 113–14, 137
  values and, 107, 110, 113–14
  visions and, 75
  see also keep, change and try; restructuring; rethinking; technological change
change agents, 91
Chantico Technical Management, 30–1
The Chaos Frontier, 16
chaos theories, 65
Chapman, A., 101
Cheng, K.M., 98
Chinese self-managing schools, 24
church groups, 127
'Client Scan Questions from Value Statements' worksheets, 209, 211
client scans, 144, 157, 162, 184, 189, 205–13

'cluster' concept, 25
Codd, J., 123
collaboration, 28, 29, 47, 57, 101, 119, 128, 132, 138, 139, 142
  see also committees-based strategic planning; group work (planning session)
collating key result areas, 156, 190–2
collating value statements, 168–70
committees, 47
committees-based strategic planning, 138–42, 144, 145–6
'common vision', 74
communication, 104, 105, 106
communities, see school communities
Competency Based Assessment and Training, 56
competency-based teaching methods, 82
competitive analysis, 32
complexity theories, 65, 66
conflict, 6, 109, 111, 212
Confucian values, 98
consensus, 29, 34, 102
consequence focused decision making, 102
consequences to megaplanning, 15
consultants, 69, 71, 101, 133, 134–5, 145
consultation, 47, 132, 133, 138, 139, 141
consultation phase, 69
content approaches, 32
contingency planning, 146
control, 7, 53, 67, 100
'Converting Values to Mission' worksheet, 172, 173
co-operation, 53
cooperative plans, 42
core values, 102, 106, 114, 129
corporate plans, 14, 42
corporate sponsorship, 58

corporate values, 107
cost-benefit analysis, 98
cost efficiency, 10, 23, 51, 53
critical issues, 143, 145, 154–5,
    161, 174–7
critical operating tasks, 79, 85–6,
    87, 88, 90
critical success factors, 79, 86, 92–4
cultural approaches to
    administration, 99–101
cultural borrowing, 112
cultural frames, 73
cultural shifts, 105
cultural values, 97–8, 108, 110,
    112–13, 119, 125
culture (organisational), 64, 82, 83,
    84, 86, 101, 105, 109, 142

Deal, T., 70–1
decentralisation, 57, 86, 112
    see also self-managing schools
decision-making
    expressed values and, 120–2
    values and, 13, 102, 103–5
    see also decentralisation
'deficit' planning model, 132–3
deficit thinking, 9–10, 11
delayering, 53
democratic nations, 128
development plans, 9, 26, 28, 41, 79
devolution of power and control, 7,
    57
differences v common values/
    shared beliefs, 34
Dimmock, C., 26
directions (planning session step),
    153, 160–2, 166, 169–70, 176,
    179–80, 186–8, 191, 195–6,
    202–3, 207–9
disadvantaged students, 57
'double high leverage initiatives',
    38–9
downsizing, 22, 53, 54, 55

draft plans, 201
Duignan, P., 64

economic rationalism, 7, 51, 136
Education Commission Report
    Number, 7, 24
educational administration and
    values, 97–101
educational outcomes, 40
educative leadership, 64–5
effective strategic planning
    principles, 41–9
emergent strategies, 128–9
employment patterns, 123–4
empowerment, 70, 73, 80, 81, 86,
    114, 212
end values, 103
enterprise bargaining, 12
entrepreneurial leadership, 87
environment issues, 90
environmental scans, 29, 100, 101,
    132, 133, 135
equality of education, 105
equality of opportunity, 121
espoused values, 116–19
evaluation, 29, 92, 133, 138, 139,
    141–2, 146, 152, 203, 204
    see also review
Evers, C., 99, 101
examinations and tests, 123
executive staff, 133, 134, 139, 140,
    146, 160
expressed values, 120–2
external directives and strategies,
    126, 127–8, 129, 130

facilitators, 159, 160, 166, 207
fear
    of planning, 21–3
    of restructuring, 51–2
The Fifth Discipline, 114
financial plans, 162
flexibility, 30, 41, 43–4, 49

focus sheets, 44, 144, 146, 156, 157, 161, 193–200
'Forming the Mission Statements' worksheet, 179
Foster, W.P., 98–9
Four Ds, 51
Framework for Innovation, 32
frameworks, 70–3, 74
framing, 53
free choice/action, 67
Fullan, M., 75, 76
future, 8, 11, 29, 40, 59, 64, 69, 142–3
see also change; critical issues

gap analysis, 10, 100, 101, 132, 133, 136–7
Garmston, R., 142
gender equity, 12
generative learning, 63, 64, 76
Giroux, H., 125
global economy, 37
global issues, 110–13
goal identification, 145
government requirements, 126–30
Greenfield, T., 12, 67, 99, 102
Gretzky, W., 16
group work (planning session)
  collating and prioritising key result areas and, 190, 192
  critical issues and, 176
  focus sheet writing and, 195
  mission statement writing and, 178, 179, 180
  values scan and, 164–5, 168–9, 170–2
growth plans, 26

Hallinger, P., 51
Hammer, M., 55
'hands off' methods, 56, 57
harassment, 12
Hargreaves, A., 28, 75, 76

Harvard policy model, 32
Herman, J., 12
Herman, J.J., 92
Herman, J.L., 82
hermeneutics, 100
'heroic' leadership, 87
hexagons, *see* planning hexagons
hierarchical structure, 52, 53, 62
high leverage initiatives, 39
Hodgkinson, C., 102
Hong Kong
  SAR of, 26
  self-managing schools of, 24, 110
  SMI and, 26–7
  values clash case study from, 119–20
Hopkins, D., 28
human resource frames, 71, 72–3
human resources
  importance of, 68–70
  valuing of, 64
  see also executive staff; parents; school communities; students; teachers and staff
Hutchinson, B., 115

The Ice Man Cometh, 21–3
identity, 58
imported strategic policy, 19
imposed values, directions and guidelines, 126–30
inclusion policies, 57
inclusiveness of value statements, 169
individual learning, 65
informal networks, 62
Ingram, B., 77
innovation, 74, 106, 116, 142
in-service management development programmes, 33
interdependence, 56, 57
interests, 58
International School Improvement Project, 28

introduction (values-based process), 154, 158–63
involvement, 169
  see also parents; teachers and staff
involvement principle, 47–8
Islamic values, 98

Jeffery, N., 199
job losses, 22, 51

Kaufman, R., 6, 9–10, 11, 12, 14, 15, 31, 40, 131
keep, change and try, 143–4, 155–6, 183–9, 192, 194, 206
Keidel, R., 52, 53
key issues, 37
key result areas, 137, 144, 156, 161, 183, 184, 185, 190–2, 194, 195, 196
key tasks, 199
Kiggundu, M., 85

labour costs, 51
Lakonski, G., 99
Landlow Primary School, 54
Langhorne, P., 113
Lau Chi Kin School, 58–9
leaders(hip), 14, 17, 23, 33, 37–8, 57, 61–77, 87, 107, 108–9, 113–14, 137, 159, 212–13
  see also executive staff
leadership frames, 71
'learning communities of practice', 62
learning culture, 64
learning organisations, 23, 53, 63–6
legislation, 12
Leithwood, K., 98, 101, 102
Lieberman, A., 52, 114
'life world', 103
lifelong learning, 124
Lim, Mrs, 4–5, 17, 43, 79, 88, 92–3, 94

logical incrementalism, 32
long-range plans, 34–5, 36
Lopes, I., 21–3

MacGilchrist, B., 42
MacPherson, R., 64
macroplanning, 14, 15, 16, 92
mainstreaming, 57
Malaysian values, 97
management committees, 140, 145, 146
Management by Objectives, 106
market-lending organisations, 68
maths, 82,
meaning, 107
megaplanning, 15, 16
metal work industry, precision, 51
microplanning, 14, 15, 16
micropolitical processes, 136
Miller, L., 52, 114
mini-schools, 57
Mintzberg, H., 30, 31, 32, 127, 128
mission statements/missions, 22, 32, 33–4, 35, 42, 58, 69, 75, 76, 86, 113, 118–19, 132, 134, 137, 143, 155, 161, 178–82
Morgan, G., 38–9
Mortimore, P., 28, 42
myths and legends, 91

National Student Profiles, 56
natural justice legislation, 12
negotiation, 145
networks/networking, 62, 72, 121
New Zealand self-managing schools, 24
norms, 13, 73, 125, 126
Northern Territory
  expressed values case study from, 121–2
  reengineering in, 55–6
notice boards, see Wall

objectives, *see* performance
indicators
objectives (planning session step),
153, 159, 166, 168–9, 175, 179,
185, 191, 194, 202, 206
occupational health and safety, 84–5
O'Donoghue, T., 26
office values worksheet sample, 167
openness, 111
operational plans, 83
see also strategies
opinion leaders, 39–40
organisational design processes,
52–9
organisational dynamism, 65
organisational perceptions, 106
organisational purpose, 57, 58–9,
105
organisational redesign, 50–6, 63
organisational reengineering, *see*
reengineering
organisational restructuring, *see*
restructuring
organisational rethinking, *see*
rethinking
organisational structures, 83, 90–2
organisational transformation, 64,
65
organisational units, 52, 53
organisational will, 67
organisations as machines, 108
outcome-based education, 106
outcome indicators, 199–200
outcomes, *see* performance
indicators
output indicators, 199–200
ownership feelings, 151–2

parents
client scans of, 144, 157, 162,
184, 189, 205–7
involvement of, 8, 9, 16, 29, 44,
48, 72, 80, 152, 159

planning process sessions and,
158, 159
values of, 11
Pascale, P., 74
paternalism, 68
patterning, 53
Patterson, J., 106, 110, 111, 119
Pedler, M., 64
people, *see* executive staff; human
resources; parents; school
communities; students; teachers
and staff
people orientation, 12–13
performance audits, 133, 135–6, 145
performance indicators, 137, 194,
195, 198–200
planning committees, 132
planning consultants, *see*
consultants
planning hexagons, 79, 81–5
planning process (values-based),
10, 16, 41–9, 151–213
planning sessions, 152–200
policy cloning, 112–13
political frames, 71, 72
pooled interdependence, 56, 57
portfolio methods, 32
position descriptions, 86
power
devolution of, 7, 57
leaders and, 114
'rolling down' model and, 69
principalship training programmes,
33
prioritising (key result areas), 156,
190–2
private sector organisation
restructuring, 54
privatisation, 24
proactivity, 37
productivity, 10, 71
professional development, 121
professional development sub-
committees, 140

profiles, 29, 56, 57
public sector organisation
  restructuring, 54
purpose
  planning session steps, 153, 159,
    165–6, 168, 171, 175, 179, 184–5,
    191, 193–4, 202, 206
  school/organisation, 57, 58–9, 105
purpose rethinking, 57, 58–9

Qantas, 67–8
quality achievement, 13

rational elements, 45
reciprocal interdependence, 56, 57
Recognition (or Accreditation) of
  Prior Learning, 56–7
reengineering, 52, 53, 55–7, 59, 63,
  136
reframing, 70–3
relevance principle, 48
repositioning, 53
representativeness of value
  statements, 169
responsibility, 145
restructuring, 22, 23, 52, 53, 54, 55,
  59, 63, 69, 99, 136, 142, 146
result areas, key, 29
results orientation, 12, 13
rethinking, 52, 53, 57–9, 63, 136
retrenchment, 54, 99
review, 44, 92, 146, 203
  see also evaluation
rhetorical plans, 42
rightsizing, 53, 54
The Rise and Fall of Strategic
  Planning, 31
risk management, 83, 84, 85
role
  of consultants, 101
  of families, 57
  of leaders, 61–3, 64–5
  of parents, 57

of school, 27, 41
of strategic planning, 11
of values in planning, 99
'rolling down' model, 68–9
Rost, J., 114

St Andrew's Secondary School, 4–5,
  84, 85
Saul, P., 74
Schlechty, P., 52
Schon, D., 65, 105
school charters, 27
school communities, 7, 54, 63, 73,
  80, 106, 107, 108, 114, 125, 126,
  145, 151, 152, 157, 158, 159, 162,
  202, 208
  see also client scans; parents;
    students; teachers and staff
School Councils, 86
school improvement, 23, 114, 115
school improvement guide, 7–9
school improvement plans, 5, 7,
  26, 27–30, 42, 43, 52
school leaders, see leaders(hip)
School Management Initiative,
  26–7, 110
school purpose, 57, 58–9
school timetables, 86
school values and beliefs, 41, 48, 49,
  50, 63, 75, 102–3, 105, 107–10, 114,
  116–17, 126–30, 179, 209–10
school values worksheet sample,
  167–8
school work plans, 27
'Schools of the Future', 27
science, 82
scientific management approaches,
  66, 67, 98–9, 100–1
  see also traditional strategic
    planning processes
Scott, R., 45
self-managing schools, 7, 23, 24–6,
  42, 110, 112, 115, 124, 128

Semler, R., 132
Senge, P., 64, 114–15
sequential collaboration, 29
sequential interdependence, 56, 57
Sergiovanni, T., 14, 102–3, 105–6, 109, 116
seven planning hexagons, *see* planning hexagons
shared values, 102, 103, 105–6, 114–16
shared vision, 114–15
shareholders, 53
Simon, H., 66
simplicity principle, 48–9
Singapore
  mission statements and, 33–4, 42
  school work plans of, 27
  self-managing schools in, 24–5
  values in, 97
singular plans, 42
Smyth, J., 25, 114
social accountability, 102
social class, 125
social reality, 65
socialisation of students, 122–6
Southeast Asia, 97–8
Special Administrative Region, 26
Spinks, J., 25
stability, 80
Stacey, R., 16, 34, 37, 74
staff, *see* executive staff; teachers and staff
staff development planning, 92
staff histories, 91
stakeholder management approaches, 32
stakeholders, 29, 45, 48, 49, 54, 74, 114, 132
standards, 103
Stanton, S., 55
Starrat, R., 107
steering committee, 139
Stoll, L., 28, 29
Stott, K., 33–4, 42

strategic advantage, 53
strategic choice, 31–9
strategic development, 133, 137–8, 139, 141
strategic directions, 100, 133, 137, 139, 140–1, 146
strategic goals, 195, 196
'strategic issue agendas', 37
strategic issues management, 32
strategic management tasks, 79, 86–7, 88, 90–2
strategic negotiations, 32
strategic plan document, 202, 203
strategic plan working party, 201–2, 203
strategic planning cycle, 203
strategic planning defined, 30–1, 49, 50
strategic planning implementation, 42–9
strategic planning requirements, 26–7
strategic planning systems, 32
strategic thinking, 78–96
strategies, 138
  see also operational plans
structural frames, 71
structures, *see* organisational structures
students
  disadvantage and, 57
  planning involvement and, 8, 29
  socialisation of, 122–6
  values of, 122–6, 128
sub-committees, 140, 145
subjectivity, 136
success (planning session step), 153, 159–60, 166, 169, 175–6, 179, 185–6, 191, 194–5, 202, 206–7
surveys, *see* client scans
survival, 53, 64
survival learning, 64
SWOT analysis, 132, 135

symbolic frames, 71
system requirements, 26–7
systems analyses, 101
systems theory, 67

tactical competitiveness, 53
teachers and staff
  accountability of, 98
  change and, 23, 44, 46, 175
  client scans and, 205–7, 209
  committees and, 140
  emergent and divergent strategies
    and, 128–9
  expressed values case study and,
    120–2
  frames and, 72
  involvement of, 8, 9, 16, 29, 44,
    45–7, 81, 84, 100, 101, 115, 121,
    142–3, 145, 146, 152, 158, 159,
    160, 202
  leadership and, 72, 74
  plan implementation and, 78
  planning process sessions and,
    158, 159, 160, 162, 194
  strategic/corporate viewpoints
    and, 11
  strategic thinking and, 78–9, 80–1,
    82, 84, 85, 87, 88, 90, 91, 92–4,
    95–6
  traditional organisational values
    and, 108, 109, 125
  values of, 11, 107, 111, 115, 119–22,
    128, 142
  voice of, 76
  see also executive staff; human
    resources; leaders(hip)
team building activities, 33
team management, 57
team teaching, 57
teamwork, 70, 94, 120
  see also group work (planning
    session)
technical frames, 71–2

technological change, 51, 69
telephone client scans, 205–7, 209,
  210
telling and selling, 165
theory of operation, 103–5
'think results' mentality, 12
Thousand, J., 108
time-out-desk, 82
top-down decisions, 10, 11, 15, 31,
  47, 48, 77, 113, 114, 124–5, 131,
  133–8, 144, 145–6, 147
Total Quality Management, 106
'Towards Excellence in Education',
  24, 27
Towards the 90s, 55
Towards the 21st Century, 52
traditional organisational values,
  107–10, 125
traditional strategic planning
  processes, 132–42, 144, 145–6,
  147
transformational effects, 64
transformational leadership, 106, 137
try, *see* keep, change and try
Tung Low Secondary School, 52

UK self-managing schools, 24, 25
universal values, 107–8
unknowability, 36
US self-managing schools, 24
useful advice (planning session
  step), 153, 162, 167, 170, 172,
  176, 180, 188, 196, 203–4, 209

value conflicts, 109, 119–20, 126,
  127, 129
'value-free' people planning, 99,
  100, 101
value judgments, 99
value shifts, 105, 120
value statements, 121, 122, 126,
  161, 164, 165–70, 171–2, 177,
  181, 182, 209

values based strategic planning, 4, 17–18, 142–4, 145–6, 147, 151–213

values based strategic planning steps, 151–213

values and beliefs, 11, 13–14, 23, 29, 34, 40–1, 48, 49, 58–9, 65, 66, 67–8, 69, 73, 75, 76, 86, 90, 92, 97–130, 137, 143, 168, 170–2, 209–10

values cards, 168–70, 171–2

values defined, 102–5

values-driven schools, 105–7, 110

values establishment, 165–6

'Values to Mission' worksheet, 179, 181

values scanning, 91, 143, 154, 164–73

Villa, R., 108

vision, 32–3, 34, 35, 36, 69, 73–7, 113, 114–15, 118–19, 137

vision statements, 132, 134, 137

visionary leaders, 68–9

voice, 76–7

Walker, A., 33–4, 42

Walker, B., 109

The Wall, 208–9

Wellman, B., 142

'what the school values', 40–1

Whitehouse, P., 115

wide consultation, 47

Wong, K., 98

Wong Ngai Leung, 119–20

working party, strategic plan, 201–2, 203

workplace agreements, 12

worksheets, 154, 163, 167–8, 172–3, 176, 177, 178, 179, 181–2, 183–4, 186, 187, 188–9, 197–8, 209–11